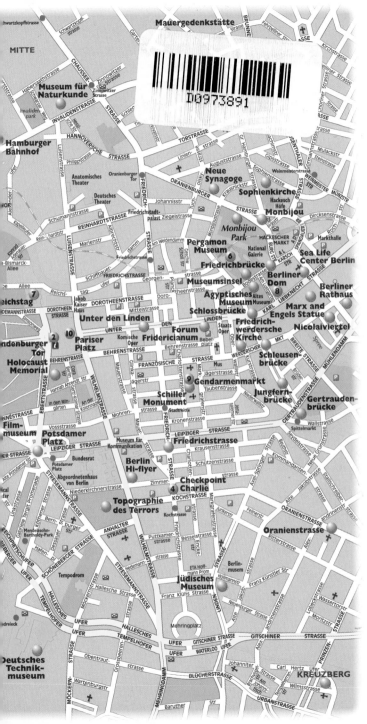

Berlin's
25Best

by Christopher Rice and Melanie Rice

Fodor's Travel Publications
New York • Toronto •
London • Sydney • Auckland
www.fodors.com

How to Use This Book

KEY TO SYMBOLS

✚	Map reference to the accompanying fold-out map	❓	Other practical information
✉	Address	▷	Further information
☎	Telephone number	ℹ	Tourist information
🕐	Opening/closing times	✋	Admission charges: Expensive (over €5), Moderate (€2.5–5), and Inexpensive (€2.5 or less)
🍴	Restaurant or café		
🚆	Nearest rail station	★ Major Sight	★ Minor Sight
Ⓜ	Nearest subway (Metro) station	👣 Walks	🚌 Excursions
🚌	Nearest bus route	🎫 Shops	
⛴	Nearest riverboat or ferry stop	🎵 Entertainment and Nightlife	
♿	Facilities for visitors with disabilities	🍽 Restaurants	

This guide is divided into four sections

• **Essential Berlin:** an introduction to the city and tips on making the most of your stay.
• **Berlin by Area:** We've broken the city into seven areas, and recommended the best sights, shops, entertainment venues, nightlife and restaurants in each one. Suggested walks help you to explore on foot.
• **Where to Stay:** the best hotels, whether you're looking for luxury, budget or something in between.
• **Need to Know:** the info you need to make your trip run smoothly, including getting about by public transport, weather tips, emergency phone numbers and useful websites.

Navigation In the Berlin by Area chapter, we've given each area of the city its own colour, which is also used on the locator maps throughout the book and the map on the inside front cover.

Maps The fold-out map accompanying this book is a comprehensive street plan of Berlin. The grid on this fold-out map is the same as the grid on the locator maps within the book. We've given grid references within the book for each sight and listing.

Contents

CONTENTS

Introducing Berlin

Berlin has certainly lived through interesting times. Decline, fall and rise again have followed each other in rapid succession since the start of the 20th century. Now, Berlin is burgeoning, blossoming— and yes, all but bankrupt. But Berlin is back.

What is Berlin? A hard city indeed to lay out in words. The capital is a reunified federal Germany, but that reveals little. A place of baleful recollection and courageous defiance, all in living memory, but that doesn't tell you much about right now. A vast studio for artists and a vast building site for entrepreneurs and government departments—that says more.

Berlin is a walk in the park through the green hectares of the Grunewald and the Tiergarten, and a constricted stroll around the grim obstacle course of the Holocaust Memorial. It is a café terrace on the banks of the Spree and a smoky Turkish coffee house in Kreuzberg; a designer-shopping expedition on the Ku'damm and a hard scrabble around the down-at-heel street market in Prenzlauer Berg; a night at the Deutsche Oper and an ear-splitting rave at a repurposed brewery now dubbed the Kultur Brauerei. It is all of these, and more. Berlin can be both *gemütlich* and hard-edged, sardonic and sentimental, cultivated and raucous, multicultural and narrow-minded (on occasion all at once). In a sense this city is still divided into East and West, this time by an invisible yet slowly fading line in its psyche.

Alternative lifestyles abound. Cabaret is going strong, and transvestite shows are legion. Visitors pour in for the Love Parade as well as for business conventions. An exuberant feeling of something new in the making still courses through the place, an energy that needs to find an outlet and Berlin has plenty of appropriate (and inappropriate) outlets.

Above all, Berlin is once again where it was destined to be: one of the great European capitals, warts and all.

Facts + Figures

- The population of Berlin is 3.6 million.
- 46% of the population is male; 54% female.
- More than 12% of the population is of foreign extraction, a third of them of Turkish origin.

HEART TRANSPLANT

A new city heart has emerged between Potsdamer Platz and the government district along the former east-west border. Completely destroyed during World War II, this area was the biggest building site in Europe during the 1990s. Today, it is a bustling entertainment and business district, reflecting Berlin's modern architectural face.

DOWNRIGHT NEIGHBOURLY

Berlin is shaped by its neighbourhoods, all with their own unique character and focus. Historically, the districts were defined according to class boundaries, but the years of division and the unification that followed have influenced the character of individual areas. There is a niche for everyone; each district has something to offer.

FRESH AIR

Nearly a third of Berlin consists of parks, meadows, woodland, lakes (Berlin is surrounded by lakes) and rivers. There are more than 16,000ha (39,500 acres) of woodland inside the city. Parks, castle grounds, zoos and botanical gardens all provide spaces to relax in and keep the city air relatively clean.

A Short Stay in Berlin

DAY 1

Morning Start the day with a stroll through the **Tiergarten** (▷ 66–67). Aim to end at the **Brandenburg Gate** (▷ 60), from where you can easily reach the **Reichstag** (▷ 65), where the federal German parliament sits.

Mid-morning Go south, taking in the grim symbology of the **Holocaust Memorial** (▷ 69) along the way, to monumental **Potsdamer Platz** (▷ 39–48). From here it's not far along Potsdamer Strasse to the **Gemäldegalerie** (▷ 42–43) for a session of serious art appreciation.

Lunch To be kind to your feet at this point, go up onto Tiergarten Strasse and take bus 200 west to Breitscheid Platz. Then cross over to **Kurfürstendamm** (▷ 33). For a light lunch, choose either **Soup-Kultur** (▷ 38), or one of the great snack bars inside the **KaDeWe** (▷ 36).

Afternoon Backtrack the short distance to Breitscheid Platz for a close-up look at the bomb-blasted **Kaiser-Wilhelm-Gedächtniskirche** (▷ 32), and pass a few moments in quiet contemplation in its memorial chapel.

Mid-afternoon Either walk via side streets, or take bus 145 northwest to Luisenplatz. This places you to visit ornate **Schloss Charlottenburg** (▷ 24–25). Before doing so, look in at the **Keramik-Museum** (▷ 26).

Dinner Multiple public transport options can take you all the way to Mitte at **Unter Den Linden** (▷ 68). German dining should be on your agenda for the first day; **Dressler** (▷ 72) is a good mid-range choice.

Evening Continue the evening at the **Deutsche Oper** (▷ 27) or the **Schauspielhaus** (▷ 71), or take in some alternative theatre at the **Maxim Gorki Theater** (▷ 71).

DAY 2

Morning Start out at the corner of **Friedrichstrasse** (▷ 61) and Kochstrasse to take in that Cold War-era Berlin Wall sight, Checkpoint Charlie. Head up Friedrichstrasse, and pop into French-owned department store **Galeries Lafayette** (▷ 70) on the way. At Unter den Linden turn right. Next to the **Staatsoper** (▷ 71) is the **Opernpalais Unter den Linden Café** (▷ 72), where you can have a coffee or breakfast.

Mid-morning Cross the River Spree to the **Museumsinsel** (▷ 78–79), thickly clustered with stellar museums to choose from.

Lunch You can go to one of the museum cafés for lunch; leave the Museumsinsel and take in some American diner munchies on the far side of **Monbijou Park** (▷ 82), at **Sixties** (▷ 86).

Afternoon Stroll around some of the alternative galleries in and around the **Hackesche Höfe** (▷ 46, 85), before crossing Karl-Liebknecht-Strasse to the **Marx and Engels Memorial** (▷ 82) to wonder what the founders of Communism would have made of it all.

Mid-afternoon Take some time to explore **Alexanderplatz** (▷ 73), the heart of the old East Berlin. Take the elevator to the top of the Fernsehturm for an unparalleled view over the city.

Dinner Take the U-Bahn two stops to Senefelderplatz and walk the short distance to **Kollwitzplatz** (▷ 90) and adjacent Wörther Strassse, to dine at the great Thai restaurant **Mao Thai Stammhaus** (▷ 94).

Evening Since you are now in trendy Plenzlauer Berg, why not take in some dance and music action at the **Kesselhaus** (▷ 93).

Top 25

▶▶▶

Alexanderplatz ▷ 76 This historic square has been transformed into a bustling meeting place.

Bauhaus-Archiv ▷ 44 Simplicity and functionalism are expressed by the Bahaus school of design.

Bergmannstrasse ▷ 52 This major street encompasses the multiethnic face of the Kreuzberg district.

Zoologischer Garten ▷ 34 One of the world's most important zoos, with outdoor enclosures creating a sense of openness.

Unter den Linden ▷ 68 Fine buildings and superb statues in the former heart of imperial Berlin.

Tiergarten ▷ 66–67 A peaceful haven in the heart of the city with ornamental gardens, lakes and wooded areas to explore.

Spandau Zitadelle ▷ 100 An attractive village with an ancient fortress on the rivers Havel and Spree.

Schloss Charlottenburg ▷ 24–25 Explore this lavish royal palace and its riverside grounds.

Reichstag ▷ 65 Visit the spectacular glass dome of the German parliament building.

Pergamon Museum ▷ 81 Houses the city's impressive collection of archaeological discoveries.

Pariser Platz ▷ 64 A handsome monumental square that's at the heart of Berlin.

Oranienstrasse ▷ 53 Buzzing with life, this long street is the soul of 'alternative' Kreuzberg.

These pages are a quick guide to the Top 25, which are described in more detail later. Here they are listed alphabetically and the tinted background shows which area they are in.

Berliner Dom ▷ 77 The highly decorated dome of Berlin's Protestant cathedral is accessible to the public.

Brandenburger Tor ▷ 60 The city's last remaining city gate is Berlin's most symbolic landmark.

Ethnologisches Museum ▷ 98 The collection covers pemanent displays from Oceania and the Americas.

Friedrichstrasse ▷ 61 This shopping street is also home to theatres, restaurants and bars.

Gemäldegalerie ▷ 42–43 This small gallery holds some 2,700 European paintings from the 13th to the 18th centuries.

Gendarmenmarkt ▷ 62–63 This lovely square is bounded by a museum, a theatre and two cathedrals.

Husemannstrasse ▷ 91 This is a newly hip area, along with Kollwitzplatz.

Jagdschloss Grunewald ▷ 99 This hunting lodge, now a museum, is situated in a forest west of the city.

Kaiser-Wilhelm-Gedächtniskirche ▷ 32 These stark ruins are a monument to the horrors of war.

Kollwitzplatz ▷ 90 Around this street, Prenzlauer Berg is humming with life and energy.

Kurfürstendamm ▷ 33 The bustling Ku'damm has a diverse array of shops and entertainment venues.

PRENZLAUER BERG 87–94
Volkspark Humboldthain
Mauerpark
Husemannstrasse
Kollwitzplatz
MITTE
Invalidenpark
UNTER DEN LINDEN 57–72
ALEXANDERPLATZ 73–86
Pergamon Museum
Moabijou Park
Alexanderplatz
Museumsinsel
Reichstag
Unter den Linden
Berliner Dom
Brandenburger Tor
Pariser Platz
Spree
Nicolaiviertel
Tiergarten
Gendarmenmarkt
Gemäldegalerie
Friedrichstrasse
POTSDAMER PLATZ 39–48
Oranienstrasse
KREUZBERG
KREUZBERG 49–56
Bergmannstrasse
Viktoriapark

Nikolaiviertel ▷ 80 An old quarter with cobbled streets and arcades filled with craft and gift shops.

Museumsinsel ▷ 78–79 Museum Island is home to some of Berlin's finest museums.

Shopping

Berlin has plenty to offer shoppers and the city is increasingly trading on its consumer appeal to attract visitors. You can buy everything here from designer labels and luxury jewellery to chic furniture and unusual gifts.

Retail Therapy

Brand shoppers and designer-label fans will be at home among names such as Gucci, Cerruti, Yamamoto and Diesel on Friedrichstrasse. The Kurfürstendamm in the west of the city also has its fair share of the big names, including Versace and Gaultier. There are more than a dozen department stores in the city catering to all tastes and trends. The upmarket KaDeWe (Kaufhaus des Westens) just off the Ku'damm, with a seemingly inexhaustible array of merchandise on six floors, is the largest. Galeries Lafayette off Friedrichstrasse has a fantastic food hall in the basement and the Arkaden in Potsdamer Platz has a wide selection of well-known brands on all three floors, with a great selection of restaurants and cafés on the top floor, ideal for relaxing and refuelling.

Individual Style

For something a little less mainstream, head for the weird and wonderful shops around Oranienburger Strasse in Mitte, Bergmannstrasse and Oranienstrasse in Kreuzberg and Golzstrasse in Schöneberg for bizarre shoes and bags, crazy clothes and trendy shades and jewellery. Off the beaten track, spend an afternoon window-shopping or pick up some unusual items in some of the off-beat shops around Kreuzberg and Prenzlauer

SECOND-HAND

Trendsetters in this style-conscious capital are not afraid to celebrate the past. There are many retro and alternative clothing outlets around Prenzlauer Berg, but if you are serious about second-hand shopping head for the larger outlets such as Colours and Garage (▷ 36) where you buy clothing by the kilo.

From confectionery and sausages to fashion and souvenirs, Berlin sells it all

Berg. Kastanienallee in Prenzlauer Berg is the heart of Berlin's alternative fashion scene where you will find funky accessories, gifts and quirky up-and-coming designer boutiques.

East and West

There are plenty of shops selling DDR memorabilia and clothing. A daily market in Alexanderplatz sells the genuine army uniforms and badges, but shops around Hackescher Markt and Prenzlauer Berg sell retro and cult clothing, accessories and souvenirs paying tribute to the city's history. Look out for souvenirs and clothing bearing the *Ampelmann* logo, the green-and-red-hat-wearing man seen at stop signs in the former east of the city. Other unique purchases include homemade chocolates found in tempting confectionery shops around the city and fine royal porcelain, both recent and antique items, made by KPM. Also find a traditional bakery and sample Germany's delicious individual breads.

Malls

On days when the weather is simply too bad to be out on the street shopping, head for one of the big malls instead. For mainstream shopping, the Europa Center on Tauentziestrasse, the Uhland-Passage and the Kempinski Plaza on Uhlandstrasse, are all central and have plenty of choice. Out east there's the Berliner Markthalle on Rosa-Luxembourg-Strasse.

Beer tankards (top). Designer gear in a chic store (middle). Puppets in a Munich toy shop (bottom)

MARKETS

Berlin has a huge number of flea markets selling clothing, jewellery and antiques. For surprising finds head for the antiques market (Wed–Mon) on Georgenstrasse under the S-Bahn bridge. You can pick up some exotic bargains at the Turkish Market on Kollwitzplatz on Thursday afternoons. Weekly street markets are a great place to experience the multicultural tastes of the city. The Winterfeldplatz market on Wednesday and Saturday morning is the best. Mingle among the friendly crowd and sample some Turkish, Italian and Greek delicacies.

Shopping by Theme

Whether you're looking for a department store, a quirky boutique, or something inbetween, you'll find it all in Berlin. On this page shops are listed by theme. For a more detailed write-up, see the individual listings in Berlin by Area.

Berlin by Night

Berlin's nightlife was once all but legendary. With the pangs of war, deprivation, division and reunification fading into the past, the city is abuzz with new life at all points on the after-dusk spectrum.

24-Hour Party

Nightlife continues well into the morning in Berlin as there are no licensing hours restricting opening time. Things don't really get going until after midnight, but the latest place to meet before the party starts is the after-work club, where lounges encourage you to wind down and relax before you hit the town.

Clubs

Berlin's club scene is split into two categories: institutions that have stood the test of time and single occasion parties playing the latest sounds publicized via word of mouth within the extremely prolific undergound scene. It is worth tracking down one of the best clubs in Berlin, the legendary WMF club, which moves to different venues. Established clubs are probably the best bet, and there is plenty of choice, but you should check out the latest listings as most have diverse offerings and certain nights may not be to your taste.

Performance

The cultural scene in Berlin ranges from traditional opera houses and cabarets to experimental theatre, live jazz and new metal bands, with something to cater for all tastes.

By night Berlin is an illuminated wonder of modern and Romanesque architecture

LISTINGS

Useful listings magazines include *Prinz, Tip, Zitty* (all twice-monthly, in German); *Berlin TutGut* (from Tourist Information, in English); *Berlin Das Magazin* (quarterly, in English and German); *Berlin Programm* (monthly, in German). *Prinz* also publishes an annual magazine picking out the best restaurants, shops, bars, clubs and hotels in the city. Berlin Tourismus Marketing publishes *Berlin-Kalendar* every two months in English and German.

Eating Out

Sure, Berlin is a great place for trying all kinds of traditional, regional German cuisine. But increasing cosmopolitanism, wealth and confidence has spawned a wave of new and varied dining experiences.

Breakfast

Bakeries (*Bäckereien*) serve an array of pastries, cakes and coffees, and sometimes rolls and sandwiches. Many bakeries also have a small seating or standing area for 'eating in'.

Snacks

Snack bars (*Imbissstuben*) usually serve a few varieties of sausage in a bread roll, and may also offer fries, burgers and kebabs. Most have a standing area. Cafés often open as early as 7 or 8am, and tend to serve light snacks and hot and cold fast food, in addition to *Kaffee und Kuchen* (coffee and cakes).

Mealtime

Bistros and restaurants are generally serving by midday. In bistros you can have a coffee or a cocktail with your food while restaurants serve meals in a more conventional order with a similar range of beverages. Beer halls (*Brauhäuser*) are the places to try traditional food and sample the local beer, which is generally brewed on the premises. Vegetarians should look for the words '*vegetarische Gerichte*' (vegetarian dishes) on the menu. In beer halls it's difficult to find a dish that doesn't include meat or meat stock.

CHILDREN'S FOOD

German children eat out with their parents from an early age, particularly in beer halls (*Brauhäuser*), which during the day and in the early evening are often patronized by the whole family. Smaller portions are offered as *Kinderteller*. The food is often of the omelette or burger-and-fries variety, but if they (or you) are a bit more adventurous, starters or smaller portions of main meals are ideal. Even small children won't look out of place in many bars and restaurants before 7 or 8pm.

From street cafés to sophisticated restaurants, Berlin offers a plethora of dining experiences

Restaurants by Cuisine

There are restaurants to suit all tastes and budgets in Berlin. On this page they are listed by cuisine. For a more detailed description of each restaurant, see Berlin by Area.

GERMAN

Dressler (▷ 72)
Henne (▷ 56)
Kaisersaal (▷ 48)
Kartoffel Kiste (▷ 38)
Luisen-Bräu (▷ 28)
Lutter & Wegner (▷ 72)
Marjellchen (▷ 38)
Offenbach-Stuben (▷ 94)
Schnitzelei (▷ 28)
Vau (▷ 72)
Weinstein (▷ 94)

AUSTRIAN

Austria Brasserie (▷ 38)
Diener (▷ 38)

FRENCH

Alt Luxemburg (▷ 28)
Borchardt (▷ 72)
Café de France (▷ 72)

ITALIAN

Ana e Bruno (▷ 28)
Bocca di Bacco (▷ 72)
Casolare (▷ 56)
Ossena (▷ 56, 86)
Oxymoron (▷ 86)
Trattoria Paizza Rosso
     (▷ 86)
Die Zwölf Apostel (▷ 72)

MIXED EUROPEAN

Bamberger Reiter (▷ 38)
Funkturm (▷ 28)
Globe (▷ 48)

Gourmetrestaurant
     Lorenz Facil (▷ 48)
Hugos (▷ 38)
Mare Bê (▷ 86)
Margaux (▷ 72)
Soda (▷ 94)
Vivo (▷ 48)
Wintergarten (▷ 38)

RUSSIAN

Pasternak (▷ 94)

SPANISH

Lafil (▷ 86)

AMERICAN

The Sixties (▷ 86)

CHINESE

Aroma (▷ 28)

THAI

Mao Thai (▷ 94)

INDIAN

Amrit (▷ 56)

SINGAPOREAN

Mirchi (▷ 86)

TURKISH

Hitit (▷ 28)

MIDDLE EASTERN

Klein Istanbul (▷ 28)
Merhaba (▷ 56)
Sufissimo (▷ 56)

CAFÉS

Café Aedes-West (▷ 38)
Café Bravo (▷ 86)
Café Einstein (▷ 48)
Café e Gelato (▷ 48)
Café Übersee (▷ 56)
Café am Ufer (▷ 56)
Daily Coffee (▷ 48)
Opernpalais Unter den
     Linden (▷ 72)
Soup-Kultur (▷ 38)
Tim's Canadian Deli
     (▷ 48)
Zum Nussbaum (▷ 86)

If You Like...

However you'd like to spend your time in Berlin, these top suggestions should help you tailor your ideal visit. Each sight or listing has a fuller write-up in Berlin by Area.

CHIC SHOPPING

Bleibgrün (▷ 36): If it's good enough for Paris…
Jil Sander (▷ 36): The right form in German fashions.
KaDeWe (▷ 36): For the best of just about everything.
Fassbender & Rausch (▷ 70): The chocolates here really are wicked.

UN-CHIC SHOPPING

Berliner Zinnfiguren (▷ 36): Military miniatures for the serious enthusiast.
Henry Lehmann (▷ 27): Nondesigner perfumes with a whiff of class.
Moritzplatz Flea Market (▷ 55): Even calling it 'shopping' is a bit of a stretch.
Türkischer Markt (▷ 55): The edible side of Turkish Kreuzberg.

Berliners like to keep ahead of fashion (top). Café culture is thriving in this vibrant city (middle and bottom)

LOCAL CUISINE

Henne (▷ 56): Anything you want, so long as it's roast chicken.
Luisen-Bräu (▷ 28): Brewery restaurant with its own liquid accompaniment.
Schnitzelei (▷ 28): The fresh taste of the Alps.
Marjellchen (▷ 38): Tastes of the East (of Germany).

BEST OF ABROAD

Ana e Bruno (▷ 28): Modern Italian classics.
Gourmetrestaurant Lorenz Facil (▷ 48): Mediterranean airs and graces.
Merhaba (▷ 56): Real Anatolian ambience in Kreuzberg.
Sixties (▷ 86): Great burgers 'n' fries—what else?—US-style

Many hotels retain classic features (top). Take in some Blues at one of the city's jazz clubs (below)

HOTELS OF CHARACTER

Grand Hotel (▷ 112): The best of Berlin.
Hansablick (▷ 110): Works of art and views of the Spree.
Luisenhof (▷ 111): Housed in a restored building dating from 1822.
Savoy Hotel-Pension (▷ 111): Fine baroque columns feature here.

HOT AND COOL

A-Trane Jazz Club (▷ 37): Noteworthy modern jazz.
Chez Nous (▷ 37): Gender lines are blurred at this renowned transvestite show.
Kesselhaus (▷ 93): Dance the night away in brewery (that, sad to relate, is closed).
Pomp, Duck & Circumstance (▷ 55): Cabaret theatre that's not for the faint-hearted.

ENTERTAINING YOURSELF

Berliner Ensemble (▷ 71): Bertolt Brecht set the stage here.
Cinestar IMAX (▷ 47): BIG-screen action at the Sony Center.
Deutsche Oper (▷ 27): None but the finest notes and steps.
Philharmonie (▷ 47): Ultra-modern home base of the Berlin Philharmonic Orchestra.

A striking modern mosaic greets visitors at the reception of the Hotel Transit

LOOKING FOR A BARGAIN

Hotel Transit Loft (▷ 109): Better-than-average class and facilities.
Treat yourself to a terrace coffee at the Café am Ufer (▷ 56).
You might just pick up that valuable antique for a song at the Trödelmarkt-Strasse des 17. Juni (▷ 36).
With a public transport *Tageskarte*, take a 'cruise' on the Wannsee-Kladow ferry (▷ 107).

The minimalist bar and reception area of the Hotel Transit in Prenzlauer Berg (left)

PAMPERED LIFESTYLES

Experience heaven on a plate at the
Bamberger Reiter (▷ 38).
Galerie Pels-Leusden (▷ 36): Bargain-
basement art not to be expected.
Indulge yourself at the
Kempinski Hotel Bristol (▷ 112).
Schloss Sanssouci (▷ 104):
How Prussian royalty lived it up.

*Relax and be pampered
(top). Designer Carl
Langhans' Brandenburger
Tor (below)*

ACTVITIES FOR KIDS

Filmpark Babelsberg (▷ 101): Go
behind the scenes at a movie studio.
Sealife Center Berlin (▷ 83): Into the
depths of the underwater world.
Zeiss-Grossplanetarium (▷ 106):
See the stars in their eyes.
Zoologischer Garten (▷ 34): Visit
the zoo and aquarium here.

WORLD WAR II SITES

Brandenburger Tor (▷ 60), where the Nazis
held triumphal military processions.
Gedenkstätte Deutscher Widerstand (▷ 45),
at the headquarters of the army officers who led
the failed 1944 July Plot against Hitler.
Holocaust memorial (▷ 69): A monument to
the 6 million Jewish victims of the Nazi terror.
Kaiser-Wilhelm-Gedächtniskirche (▷ 32):
Pass a few moments in quiet contemplation at
this bombed-out cathedral.

REVISITING THE COLD WAR

Checkpoint Charlie, with an adjacent surviving
section of the Berlin Wall (▷ 61).
The Glienicker Bridge (▷ 105), where spies
were swapped.
Marx and Engels monument (▷ 82),
dedicated to the founders of
Communism.
Rathaus Schöneberg (▷ 35), where
President Kennedy famously said: 'Ich
bin ein Berliner'.

*Signs remain from the
Cold War days at
Checkpoint Charlie
(above)*

*The Glienicker Bridge is now the principal
border crossing point into Germany*

Berlin by Area

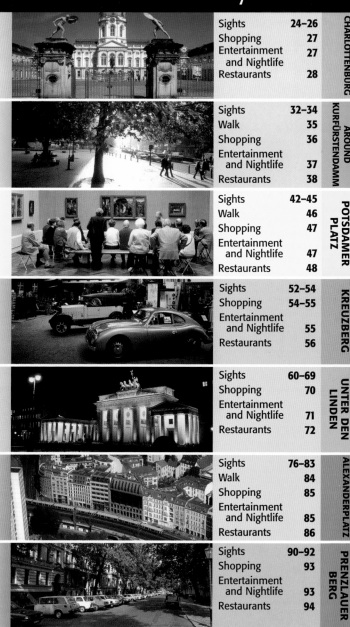

Charlottenburg

The leafy, western district of Charlottenburg is immersed in its own pursuit of the good life, with opulent Schloss Charlottenburg the most obvious stellar attraction of a quarter that is wealthy and self-assured.

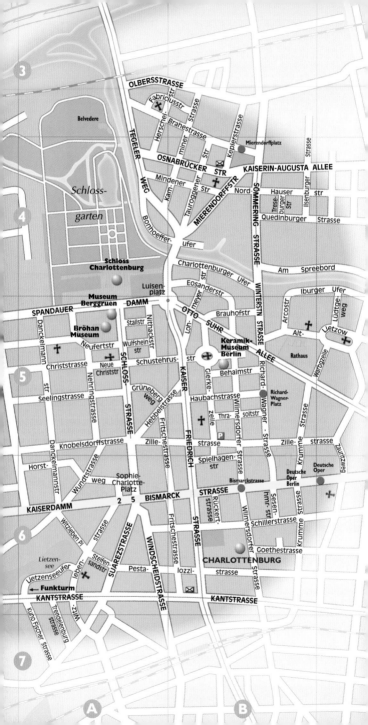

Schloss Charlottenburg

HIGHLIGHTS

- White Hall
- Golden Gallery
- Gobelins' rooms
- Study and bedchamber of Frederick I
- *Embarkation for Cythera*, J-A Watteau
- Statue of the Great Elector
- Schinkel Pavilion
- Great Orangery
- Gardens

BEHIND THE SCENES

Try to make time to join the guided tour (extra cost) of the opulent private apartments of King Friedrich I and Queen Sophie Charlotte.

This attractive former royal palace, built in the rococo style, lies in grounds only a stone's throw from the heart of Berlin. The highlights of the Schloss itself have to be the gorgeous White Hall and Golden Gallery, in the New Wing.

Royal retreat The Schloss was built over more than 100 years, and its development mirrors the aggrandisement of the Prussian dynasty of Hohenzollern, recalled in the forecourt by Andreas Schlüter's superb equestrian statue of the Great Elector, which once stood outside the Berlin Schloss. The Electress Sophie Charlotte's rural retreat—this suburb of Berlin was still deep in the countryside and considered suitable for a summer palace—designed by Arnold Nering in 1695, was transformed into the palace you see today during

This restored Prussian palace was built as a summer retreat for Queen Charlotte (left). Decoration on the palace entrance gates (top right). The Galerie der Romantik on the ground floor has a collection of 19th-century artists' work including Heinrike Dannecker by Schick (middle) and Landscape with Apollo by Philip Hackert (right)

the reigns of Frederick I and Frederick II by the architect Georg Wenzeslaus von Knobelsdorff. The Great Orangery and Theatre form wings of the palace, as does the Langhans Building, now the Museum of Pre- and Early History.

Riverside grounds Do not leave Schloss Charlottenburg without seeing the delightful grounds, which slope towards the River Spree. The formal French garden is a marked contrast to the landscaped English garden, which houses the Mausoleum built for Queen Luise, and the Belvedere, now a museum devoted to Berlin porcelain. Closer to the palace, do not miss the delightfully idiosyncratic Neue Pavilion, designed by Berlin's best-known 19th-century architect, Karl Friedrich Schinkel. Today the palace gardens are a popular public park.

THE BASICS

➕ A4

✉ Spandauer Damm 20–24

☎ 030 32 09 14 40

🕐 Altes Schloss: Tue–Sun 9–5. Neue Flügel: Apr–end Oct Tue–Sun 10–5, Nov–end Mar Tue–Sun 11–5

🍴 Restaurant

🚇 U-Bahn Richard-Wagner-Platz, Sophie-Charlotte-Platz

🚌 Bus 109, 145, 309

♿ Few

💶 Moderate

More to See

BRÖHAN-MUSEUM

In 1983, Professor Karl Bröhan presented his superb collection of Jugendstil (art nouveau), and art deco and functionalism crafts to the city. The highlights of the museum are the rooms beautifully decorated in the styles of the leading designers of the period. The porcelain collection is particularly fine.

➕ A5 ✉ Schlossstrasse 1a ☎ 030 32 69 06 00 🕐 Tue–Sun 10–6 Ⓜ U-Bahn Sophie-Charlotte-Platz 🚌 Bus 109, 145, 309 ♿ Moderate

FUNKTURM

Berlin's broadcasting tower was built between 1924 and 1926 to a design by Heinrich Straumer. It reaches up 150m (492ft) above the Messegelände Congress Centre, and has a restaurant (▷ 28) at 55m (180ft), and a viewing platform at 126m (413ft) that has fine views.

➕ Off map A6 ✉ Messedamm 22 ☎ 030 30 38 29 96 🕐 Mon 10–8, Tue–Sun 10am–11pm Ⓜ U-Bahn Kaiserdamm ♿ Moderate

KERAMIK-MUSEUM BERLIN

Tucked away in a superb town house dating from 1712 on a side street not far from Schloss Charlottenburg, the Ceramic Museum is something of a labour of love. The permanent collection covers many periods, from antique to modern styles and is supported by regularly changing temporary exhibitions.

➕ B5 ✉ Schustehrusstrasse 13 ☎ 030 902 91 29 48 🕐 Sat–Mon 1–5 Ⓜ U-Bahn Richard-Wagner-Platz ♿ Expensive

MUSEUM BERGGRUEN

A stimulating exhibition of paintings and sculptures by Picasso and his contemporaries. There are some 100 pieces by Picasso, as well as works by Klee, Matisse, Braque, Giacometti and Cézanne. The Picassos include works that cover the full extent of his artistic career, both in time and in the many styles he adopted.

➕ A5 ✉ Schlossstrasse 1 ☎ 030 32 69 580 🕐 Tue–Sun 10–6 Ⓜ U-Bahn Sophie-Charlotte-Platz 🚌 Bus 109, 145, 210, X21 ♿ Moderate

The 20th-century Funkturm (left)

The Museum Berggruen has fascinating detail both on the inside with its spiral staircase (top) and the Rotunda on the outside (bottom)

Shopping

BOOKS IN BERLIN
There is a wide spectrum of English-language books to choose from here, from classical and modern fiction to history, politics, reference and travel.
⊞ C6 ✉ Goethestrasse 69 ☎ 030 313 12 33 Ⓢ S-Bahn Savignyplatz

GIPSFORMEREI SMPK
Try here for quality plaster reproductions of items from Berlin museums, such as a bust of Queen Nefertiti.
⊞ Off map, just west of A5 ✉ Sophie-Charlotten-Strasse 17–18 ☎ 030 326 76 90 Ⓒ Sat–Mon 1–5 Ⓢ S-Bahn Westend

HENRY LEHMANN
In business since 1926, this family-owned shop creates, sells over the counter and delivers worldwide moderately priced perfumes.
⊞ B6 ✉ Kantstrasse 106 ☎ 030 324 35 82 Ⓤ U-Bahn Wilmersdorfer Strasse

KÖNIGSBERGER MARZIPAN
This long-running, family confectioners is the place to go to sample some traditional German marzipan.
⊞ B6 ✉ Pestalozzistrasse 54a ☎ 030 323 82 54 Ⓤ U-Bahn Sophie-Charlotte-Platz

Entertainment and Nightlife

CAFÉ THEATER SCHALOTTE
This one-time cinema has been transformed into a venue for alternative theatre, cabaret and music, and has an excellent foyer café.
⊞ B5 ✉ Behaimstrasse 22 ☎ 030 341 14 85 Ⓤ U-Bahn Richard-Wagner-Platz

DEUTSCHE OPER BERLIN
www.deutscheoperberlin.de
The Deutsche Oper company has been staging classical and modern opera and ballet, plus symphony and chamber concerts, since 1912. Performances since World War II have been held in Fritz Bornemann's contemporary glass-fronted building. Even in the cheap seats you get a great view of the stage and can appreciate the fantastic acoustics.
⊞ B6 ✉ Bismarckstrasse 35 ☎ 030 341 02 49 Ⓒ Mon–Sat 11–1 hour before performance, Sun 10–2 and 1 hour before performance. Ⓤ U-Bahn Deutsche Oper 🚌 101, 109

WILHELM HOECK
Settle down with a foaming pilsner beer amid the smoky hubbub and venerable surroundings of this neighbourhood *Kneipe* that's been a watering hole and Charlottenburg institution since 1829.
⊞ B6 ✉ Wilmersdorfer-strasse 149 ☎ 030 341 81 74 Ⓤ U-Bahn Bismarckstrasse

DIE WÜHLMÄUSE
Generating belly laughs since the 1960s for its sardonic treatment of German political life and social mores, this renowned comedy cabaret now occupies a theatre in the 1920s modernist Amerikahaus.
⊞ Off map, west of A6 ✉ Pommernallee 2–4 ☎ 030 306 730 11 Ⓤ U-Bahn Theodor-Heuss-Platz

---

GAMES ZONE

From Charlottenburg it's a short walk west along Kaiserdamm and Heerstrasse, or take the U-Bahn to the Olympia-Stadion (Olympic Stadium) district, where the 1936 Olympics were held during the Nazi period.

Restetaurants

CHARLOTTENBURG   RESTAURANTS

PRICES

Prices are approximate, based on a 3-course meal for one person.

€€€	over €30
€€	€15–€30
€	up to €15

ALT-LUXEMBURG (€€€)

One of the best French restaurants in the city—and then there are the German and European variations. Celebrity Chef Karl Wannemacher presides over his elegant temple of taste.

➕ A6   ✉ Windscheidstrasse 31   ☎ 030 323 87 30   🕐 Mon–Sat 5pm–12   🚇 U-Bahn Sophie-Charlotte-Platz

ANA E BRUNO (€€€)

Adventurous and experimental, this restaurant goes above and beyond the Italian classics to create a modern cuisine style with a menu that changes monthly to track seasonal ingredients and dishes.

➕ Off map, west of A5   ✉ Sophie-Charlotten-Strasse 101   ☎ 030 325 71 10   🕐 Tue–Sat 6.30pm–12   🚇 U-Bahn Bismarckstrasse

AROMA (€€)

If it's dim sum you're after this is the place to go. The furnishings may be a little dated by now for a style-conscious city, but the Cantonese dishes are first class.

➕ C6   ✉ Kantstrasse 35   ☎ 030 37 59 16 28   🕐 Daily noon–3am   🚇 U-Bahn Wilmersdorfer Strasse

FUNKTURM RESTAURANT (€€)

From a point 55m (180ft) high on the Radio Tower (▷ 26), the view outside over the city is matched by 1920s-style decor inside and breezy yet refined continental cuisine and service.

➕ Off map, west of A6   ✉ Messedamm 22   ☎ 030 30 38 29 96   🕐 Tue 6–11pm, Wed–Sun 11.30–11   🚇 U-Bahn Kaiserdamm

HITIT (€€)

Traditional spicy meat and vegetarian dishes are carefully prepared by an inventive chef at this Turkish restaraunt.

TRADITIONAL FARE

In Berlin plates come piled high with the two local staples, meat (usually pork) and potatoes, often accompanied by pickled cabbage (*Sauerkraut*), peas and the ubiquitous pickle. *Buletten* (meatballs) and *Kartoffelpuffer* (tasty potato pancakes) are Berlin specialties. However, young Germans are eschewing this diet and in an increasing number of restaurants the cuisine reflects the modern taste for lighter fare.

➕ A5   ✉ Knobelsdorff-strasse 35   ☎ 030 322 45 57   🕐 Mon–Thu 5pm–12, Sun 11am–midnight   🚇 U-Bahn Sophie-Charlotte-Platz

KLEIN ISTANBUL (€€€)

This well-known establishment—considered by many locals to be the finest Turkish eatery in town—is not cheap but the food is authentic and the service is friendly.

➕ B6   ✉ Pestalozzistrasse 84   ☎ 030 883 27 77   🕐 Daily 12–12   🚇 U-Bahn Wilmersdorfer Strasse

LUISEN-BRÄU (€€)

The in-house eatery of the Luisen-Bräu brewery is committed to traditional German cooking. Naturally there's an expectation that the popular, excellent beer provides the perfect accompaniment.

➕ B4   ✉ Luisenplatz 1   ☎ 030 341 93 88   🕐 Sun–Thu 9am–1am, Fri–Sat 9am–2am   🚇 U-Bahn Richard-Wagner-Platz

SCHNITZELEI (€€)

Putting traditional Alpine cuisine—schnitzel, wurst—together in a tasteful modern-design setting might be counter-intuitive, but it works. These and other dishes are served tapas-style, and there are vegetarian options.

➕ C5   ✉ Röntgenstrasse 7   ☎ 030 34 70 27 78   🕐 Mon–Sun 4pm–12, Sun 10am–midnight   🚇 U-Bahn Richard-Wagner-Platz

The great boulevard, Kurfürstendamm, is known locally as the 'Ku'damm'. There's far more to the bustling Ku'damm district than its renowned thoroughfare, however, as a stroll into its busy 'hinterland' will confirm.

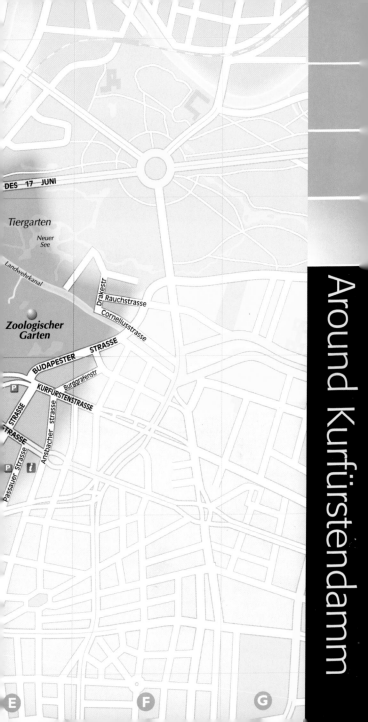

DES 17 JUNI

Tiergarten

Neuer
See

Landwehrkanal

Zoologischer
Garten

Drakestr

Rauchstrasse

Cornelliusstrasse

BUDAPESTER STRASSE

Burggrafenstr

KURFÜRSTENSTRASSE

STRASSE

Ansbacher strasse

STRASSE

Passauer Strasse

E

F

G

Kaiser-Wilhelm-Gedächtniskirche

TOP 25

The bomb-damaged original church now stands as a war memorial

THE BASICS

www.gedaechtniskirche.com
🔲 E7
✉ Breitscheidplatz
☎ 030 218 50 23
🕐 Memorial Hall: Mon–Sat 10–4. New Chapel: daily 9–7
🚇 U- or S-Bahn Zoologischer Garten, U-Bahn Kurfürstendamm
🚌 Bus 100, 109, 119, 129, 146, 200
♿ Few
🎟 Free

HIGHLIGHTS

● Cross of nails
● Surviving mosaics
● The Stalingrad Madonna
● Bell tower
● Globe Fountain

TIP

● Even if you are not particularly religious, it can be interesting to attend one of the short services (some in English) at the church.

The blackened ruin of this church—bombed in 1943, now a reminder of the cost of war—casts its shadow over the Ku'damm. Particularly moving is the cross of nails given by the people of Coventry in England, another war-torn city.

War memorial The Gedächtniskirche, built in 1895 in Romanesque style, was Kaiser Wilhelm II's contribution to the developing New West End. No expense was spared on the interior, and the dazzling mosaics are deliberately reminiscent of St. Mark's in Venice. After Allied bombs destroyed the church in 1943, the shell was allowed to stand. Poignant in its way, the old building now serves as a small museum focusing on the wartime destruction.

The New Chapel Berliners have denigrated the octagonal chapel and hexagonal stained-glass tower, both uncompromisingly modern (the 'make-up box' and the 'lipstick tube' are preferred nicknames). However, many visitors find peace in the blue-hue chapel, whose stained glass is from Chartres, France. The chapel was designed by Egon Eiermann in the early 1960s.

Breitscheidplatz In marked contrast, brash Breitscheidplatz proclaims the values of a materialistic culture, only partially redeemed by the vibrant street musicians and fund-raising stunts. Nowadays it is a refuge for Berlin's down-and-outs and is routinely targeted by the police. The focus is the Globe Fountain (Weltkugelbrunnen).

The 'Ku'damm' is the place for the latest fashions as well as chic modern art

Kurfürstendamm

It would be unthinkable to come to Berlin without visiting the 'Ku'damm', which stretches for 3km (2 miles) west towards Charlottenburg. The city's celebrated tree-lined boulevard is usually buzzing with pavement cafés, along with restaurants and Berlin's major shops.

Shopping street Many of the Ku'damm stores were the beneficiaries of the *Wirtschaftswunder*, the economic miracle of the 1960s, which was brought about partly by American investment.

New West End The elegant streets off the Ku'damm—Fasanenstrasse, for example—were part of the New West End, which was developed as a residential area at the end of the 19th century. Many of the houses here are now art galleries; an exception is the museum devoted to the life and work of the 20th-century artist Käthe Kollwitz at Fasanenstrasse 24. Next door to the museum is the Literaturhaus, a cultural hub with a secluded garden café, the Wintergarten. The Villa Grisebach at No. 25 is an outstanding example of Jugendstil architecture. On the corner of Leibnizstrasse, is another period piece, the Iduna House, whose cupola dates from 1907.

Coffee shops Johann Georg Kranzler opened the first coffee shop in Berlin in 1835, on the corner of Friedrichstrasse. Today, tourists and literati have taken the place of the Prussian aristocracy who once frequented the many cafés; join them for a superb coffee and watch the world go by.

THE BASICS

🔲 D7

🚇 U-Bahn Kurfürstendamm; U-Bahn Uhlandstrasse

🚌 Bus X10, M19, M29, 109, 110

🚉 Zoologischer Garten

Literaturhaus and Wintergarten Café
www.literaturhaus-berlin.de

🔲 D7

✉ Fasanenstrasse 23

☎ 030 887 28 60

🕐 Mon–Fri 10–5; Café daily 9.30am–1am

🍴 Excellent

♿ Few

🎟 Free

Käthe-Kollwitz-Museum
www.kaethe-kollwitz.de

🔲 D7

✉ Fasanenstrasse 24

☎ 030 882 52 10

🕐 Wed–Mon 11–6

♿ Few

🎟 Moderate

HIGHLIGHTS

● Literaturhaus
● Käthe-Kollwitz-Museum
● Fasanenstrasse
● Iduna House
● The KaDeWe department store
● Hotel Kempinski Bristol (▷ 112)
● Neoclassical newsstands

Zoologischer Garten

There's no accounting for taste—elephants enjoying a christmas tree 'snack' at the zoo

THE BASICS

www.tierpark-berlin.de
Zoo
✚ E6
✉ Hardenbergplatz 8 and Budapester Strasse 34
☎ 030 25 40 10
🕐 Daily 9–6 (closes earlier out of season) 🚇 U- or S-Bahn Zoologischer Garten
💶 Expensive. Joint ticket with Aquarium available

Aquarium
✚ E7
✉ Budapester Strasse 32
☎ 030 25 40 10
🕐 Daily 9–6
💶 Expensive. Joint ticket with Zoo available

HIGHLIGHTS

● Literaturhaus
● Giant pandas Bao Bao and Yan Yan
● Hippopotamus House
● Feeding times
● Komodo dragons in the Aquarium

Berlin's zoo has developed into one of the most important in the world, with over 14,000 animals and 1,500 species represented.

The King of Prussia The zoo dates back to 1841, when Friedrich Wilhelm IV, the King of Prussia, donated his pheasant gardens and exotic animal collection to the citizens of Berlin. After the zoo had suffered serious damage during World War II, the director, Dr. Katharina Heinroth, began the lengthy process of rebuilding it and reintroducing animals.

The zoo Moats and trenches rather than bars and cages define the outdoor enclosures, creating a sense of openness and giving visitors a good view of the animals. In the hippopotamus house glass domes cover the steamy, climate-controlled home of the Common and Pygmy hippopotamuses. A glass wall in the viewing gallery allows you to watch them swimming under water. The polar bears and seals are also free to swim around in their homes, and the seals even have their own wave machine. The stars of the zoo are the two giant pandas, Bao Bao and Yan Yan.

The Aquarium A huge statue of an Iguanodon, which became extinct 90 million years ago, guards the entrance here. The Aquarium is occupied by a variety of fish, frogs, lizards, snakes, crocodiles and turtles from all over the world. The Komodo Dragons dominate the reptile area on the second floor. Measuring 3m (10ft) in length, they are the largest lizards in the world.

A Walk: Schöneberg

Stroll through a residential district that's speckled with memories, many of them from Berlin's roller-coaster 20th-century history.

DISTANCE: 3.5km (2.2 miles) **ALLOW:** 1 hour

START

WITTENBERGPLATZ U-BAHN STATION
🚇 U-Bahn Wittenbergplatz

END

RATHAUS SCHÖNEBERG
🚇 U-Bahn Rathaus Schöneberg

① Admire the art deco interior of Wittenbergplatz station, then walk down Kleiststrasse to Nollendorfplatz, the home to the Metropol, dating from 1906 (formerly a theatre, now a nightclub).

⑦ Turn right into Grunewaldstrasse, then left into Martin-Luther-Strasse. Dominating John-F-Kennedy-Platz is the Rathaus Schöneberg, former town hall of West Berlin. It was from the balcony of this building that President Kennedy delivered his famous 'Ich bin ein Berliner' speech.

② Walk south along Maassen-strasse, crossing Nollendorfstrasse. British author Christopher Isherwood, whose reminiscences of Berlin life in the 1930s inspired the film *Cabaret*, lived at Nollendorfstrasse 17.

⑥ Just inside the park is the former Supreme Court of Justice (Kammergericht), where Count von Stauffenberg and other instigators of the failed July Bomb Plot to assassinate Hitler were tried in 1944.

③ The next square you come to, Winterfeldtplatz, has a twice-weekly market.

④ At the end of Maassenstrasse is Pallasstrasse; the Sportspalast that once stood here was the scene of many of Hitler's rallies.

⑤ Cross Pallasstrasse into Elssholzstrasse. On the left is Kleistpark, named after the Romantic poet Heinrich von Kleist, who shot himself on the shores of the Wannsee in 1811, age only 34.

Shopping

ART & INDUSTRY

Furniture, lamps and accessories in Bauhaus and other functionalist styles. Also watches.
C7 ✉ Bleibtreustrasse 40 ☎ 030 883 49 46 S-Bahn Savignyplatz

BERLINER ZINNFIGUREN

A small piece of the Prussian military tradition survives here, in exquisitely detailed, hand-painted pewter figurines of soldiers dating from ancient times up to the 19th century.
D6 ✉ Knesebeckstrasse 88 ☎ 030 315 70 00 S-Bahn Savignyplatz

BLEIBGRÜN

Cutting-edge designer fashions straight off the Paris catwalk are the stock-in-trade here.
C7 ✉ Bleibtreustrasse 30 ☎ 030 885 00 80 S-Bahn Savignyplatz

CHAPEAUX HUTMODE BERLIN

For wild but rarely woolly feminine headgear, in styles ranging from retro to frivolous to razor-sharp contemporary.
C6 ✉ Bleibtreustrasse 51 ☎ 030 312 09 13 S-Bahn Savignyplatz

DIESEL

A large shop selling the latest lines from this international brand.
D7 ✉ Kurfürstendamm 17 ☎ 030 88 55 14 53 U-Bahn Kurfürstendamm

ENERGIE STORE

Stylish retro casual wear, jeans and accessories for both sexes.
E7 ✉ Tauentzienstrasse 15 ☎ 030 23 60 99 40 U-Bahn Kurfürstendamm

GALERIE PELS-LEUSDEN

International art of the 19th and 20th centuries, displayed in the former home of turn-of-the-20th-century architect Hans Grisebach.
D7 ✉ Fasanenstrasse 25 ☎ 030 885 91 50 Mon–Fri 10–6.30, Sat 10–6 U-Bahn Uhlandstrasse

GARAGE

Second-hand clothes are sold by weight in this large warehouse near Nollendorfplatz U-Bahn station.
F7 ✉ Ahornstrasse 2 ☎ 030 211 27 60 U-Bahn Nollendorfplatz

WINTERFELDTPLATZ

One pleasant way to while away a Saturday morning is to explore the antiques shops around Motzstrasse, before homing in on one of Berlin's most vibrant and entertaining street markets, in Winterfeldtplatz. You never know quite what you will find here, which is the main attraction--everything from hand-me-down jewellery to books with faded covers, from flowers to pretty children's clothes.

JIL SANDER

Understated but eye-catching fashions from the celebrity German designer.
C7 ✉ Kurfürstendamm 185 ☎ 030 886 70 20 U-Bahn Adenauerplatz

KADEWE (KAUFHAUS DES WESTENS)

The second largest department store in the world (after Harrods of London). The wonderful Food Hall is a must. Fine city views from the top-floor café.
E7 ✉ Tauentzienstrasse 21–24 ☎ 030 212 10 Mon–Fri 10–8, Sat 9.30–8 U-Bahn Wittenbergplatz

KPM

Quality porcelain bearing the renowned hallmark of Königliche Porzellan-Manufaktur.
E5 ✉ Wegelystrasse 1 ☎ 030 39 00 90 S-Bahn Tiergarten

ROSENTHAL

Fine modern Bavarian porcelain from Rosenthal is supported by other household objects from named manufacturers.
D7 ✉ Kurfürstendamm 226 ☎ 030 885 63 40 Kurfürstendamm

TRÖDELMARKT STRASSE DES 17. JUNI

One of Berlin's largest flea markets, great for retro bargains and antiques.
E5 ✉ Tiergarten ☎ 030 26 55 00 96 Sat, Sun 10–5 S-Bahn Tiergarten

Entertainment and Nightlife

A-TRANE JAZZ CLUB
This buzzing Charlottenburg night haunt caters to lovers of modern jazz and bebop.
🔒 C6 ✉ Bleibtreustrasse 1 ☎ 030 313 25 50 🚇 S-Bahn Savignyplatz

BAR JEDER VERNUNFT
It's a long way psychologically from the anarchic watering holes of Mitte, Kreuzberg and Prenzlauer Berg, but in this bar-cum-theatre Tony Wilmersdorf has its own player, serving up drinks, music and cabaret.
🔒 D8 ✉ Schaperstrasse 24 ☎ 030 883 15 82 🚇 U-Bahn Spichernstrasse

BIG EDEN
Brought back by new owners from a near-death experience in 2002, this is once again among the coolest large dance venues in town.
🔒 D7 ✉ Kurfürstendamm 202 ☎ 030 882 61 20 🚇 U-Bahn Uhlandstrasse

CAFÉ KEESE
Something of a Berlin institution, this rather formal dance café has phones on the tables; men and women each get their chance to choose a partner.
🔒 C6 ✉ Bismarckstrasse 108 ☎ 030 312 91 11 🚇 U-Bahn Ernst-Reuter-Platz

CHEZ NOUS
Famous for its transvestite shows, and still going strong after more than 30 years. Reserve well in advance.
🔒 E7 ✉ Marburger Strasse 14 ☎ 030 213 18 10 🚇 U-Bahn Augsburger Strasse

LORETTA IM GARTEN
A beer garden that's popular with children because it has things to do, and with their parents—because it takes care of the kids.
🔒 D7 ✉ Lietzenburgerstrasse 89 ☎ 030 882 33 54 🚇 U-Bahn Uhlandstrasse

QUASIMODO
Stifling and crowded, this is a good place to hear live jazz, blues and funk. Tickets are available from 3pm on the day of performance. Live music from 10pm.
🔒 D6 ✉ Kantstrasse 12a ☎ 030 312 80 86 🚇 U- or S-Bahn Zoologischer Garten

---

GOODBYE TO CABARET

The 1920s was the undisputed golden age of cabaret, a fact seized on by Bob Fosse in his 1972 film musical *Cabaret*, based on Christopher Isherwood's novel *Goodbye to Berlin*. The main characteristics of the art form were biting political satire and unabashed sexual license. Since World War II, Berliners have done their best to revive the tradition but the modern clubs are often more like variety shows—the bite is missing.

DIE STACHELSCHWEINE
The satire (in German) at 'The Porcupines' cabaret is famously prickly and the targets widespread, both at home and abroad (watch out USA!).
🔒 E7 ✉ Europa Center, Tauentzienstrasse 9–12 ☎ 030 261 47 95 🚇 U- and S-Bahn Zoologischer Garten

THE STORY OF BERLIN
This state-of-the-art exhibition uses 3-D sound systems, touch screens, time tunnels and adventure rooms to tell the story of Berlin since 1237.
🔒 D7 ✉ Kufürstendamm 206, Ku'damm Karree ☎ 030 88 72 01 00 ⏰ Daily 10–8 🚇 U-Bahn Kufürstendamm 🚌 Bus 109, 119, 129, 219, 249 💰 Expensive (family card available)

THEATER DES WESTENS
A graceful theatre dating from 1896 is the place to go for big-budget spectacles and translations of Broadway and West End musicals.
🔒 D7 ✉ Kantstrasse 12 ☎ 030 31 90 30 🚇 U- and S-Bahn Zoologischer Garten

TIMES BAR
Named after the Times of London, the bar is a homey place to settle down in with a newspaper.
🔒 D6 ✉ Savoy Hotel, Fasanenstrasse 9–10 ☎ 030 31 10 30 🚇 U- and S-Bahn Zoologischer Garten

Restaurants

PRICES

Prices are approximate, based on a 3-course meal for one person.
€€€ over €30
€€ €15–€30
€ up to €15

AUSTRIA BRASSERIE (€€€)

Bistro with beautifully presented, Austrian and French food. Popular with businesspeople and literati.
🕂 C7 ✉ Kurfürstendamm 184 ☎ 030 881 84 61 🕐 Mon–Sun 11am–1am 🚇 U-Bahn Uhlandstrasse

BAMBERGER REITER (€€€)

Reservations are essential at this outstanding Franco-German restaurant, which makes up in fine cuisine for what its setting lacks in style.
🕂 E8 ✉ Regensburgerstrasse 7 ☎ 030 21 96 63 55 🕐 Mon–Sat 6pm–11pm 🚇 U-Bahn Spichernstrasse

DIENER (€€)

You are guaranteed to get a warm welcome at this homey old-style Berlin pub serving top-notch Austrian cuisine.
🕂 C6 ✉ Grolmanstrasse 47 ☎ 030 881 53 29 🕐 Daily 6pm–3am 🚇 S-Bahn Savignyplatz

HUGOS (€€€)

The haute cuisine prepared by Chef Thomas Kammeier has been awarded 1 Michelin star—one of only a few of Berlin's restaurants to receive the accolade. Worth it for the splendid panoramic views over Berlin from the roof.
🕂 F6 ✉ In Hotel InterContinental, Budapester Strasse 2 ☎ 030 26 02 12 63 🕐 Mon–Sat 6pm–10.30 🚇 S- and U-Bahn Zoologischer Garten

KARTOFFEL KISTE (€€€)

Tuck into wholesome and hearty German cooking at this warm restaurant dedicated to the humble potato. Every dish contains potato in some shape or form, and that includes the pizza bases.
🕂 E7 ✉ Europa-Center 1, Etage ☎ 030 261 42 54 🕐 Mon–Fri 12–10pm, Sat–Sun 12–11pm 🚇 S- and U-Bahn Zoologischer Garten

AT THE WÜRSTCHENBUDE

Sausage stands (*Würstchenbuden*) and snack bars (*Schnellimbisse*) are popular in Germany, and usually offer *Thüringer Bratwurst* (grilled sausage), the spicier *Krakauer* and *Frankfurter Bockwurst* and *Currywurst* (fried sausage with curry ketchup). Other snacks include hamburger meat balls, served hot or cold, and called *Buletten* in Berlin.

Cafés

CAFÉ AEDES-WEST (€€)

A trendy spot in a modern-architecture gallery, for those who want to see and be seen.
🕂 C7 ✉ S-Bahnbogen 559, off Savignyplatz ☎ 030 31 50 95 35 🕐 Mon–Fri 8am–midnight, Sat, Sun 9am–midnight 🚇 S-Bahn Savignyplatz

MARJELLCHEN (€€)

It's hard to experience more traditional dining than at this much-loved local institution, which specializes in the hearty dishes of Germany's lost eastern lands.
🕂 B7 ✉ Mommsenstrasse 9 ☎ 030 883 26 76 🕐 Mon–Sun 5–11.30pm 🚇 U-Bahn Adenauerplatz

SOUP-KULTUR (€)

The last word in snacks and tasty soups.
🕂 D7 ✉ Kurfürstendamm 224 ☎ 030 88 62 92 82 🕐 Mon–Sat noon–7.30pm, Sat noon–6pm 🚇 U-Bahn Kurfürstendamm

WINTERGARTEN (€–€€)

An elegant city mansion dating from 1889 is the setting for both the Literaturhaus and its fine continental-style café-restaurant. In summer tables are also set outside in the garden.
🕂 D7 ✉ Literaturhaus, Fasanenstrasse 23 ☎ 030 882 54 14 🕐 Daily 9.30am–1am 🚇 U-Bahn Kurfürstendamm

Squeezed between the southern rim of the Tiergarten and the waters of the Landwehrkanal, the district around Potsdamer Platz boasts a number of notable museums and war memorials.

5

6

TIERGARTENSTRASSE

Rauch-

strasse

STÜLERSTRASSE

KINGELHÖFERSTR

Köbisstrasse

Cornelliusstrasse

Hiroshimastrasse

Hildebrandstrasse

**Kupferstich-
kabinett**

Sigismundstr

BUDAPESTER STRASSE

Burggrafenstr

Keith-

strasse

Landgrafenstrasse

Wichmann-

strasse

Lützowufer

SCHILLSTRASSE

VON DER HEYDT

STRASSE

**Bauhaus-
Archiv**

LÜTZOWUFER

Lützow-
platz

**Gedenkstätte
Deutscher
Widerstand**

Stauffenbergstrasse

Hitzigallee

**Gemäld
galer**

REICHPIETSCHUFER

Landwehrkanal

SCHÖNEBERGER

LÜTZOWSTRASSE

UFER

Theater

Genthiner Strasse

Kluckstrasse

SCHÖNEBERGER

7

8

0   250 m

0   250 yds

F

G

Gemäldegalerie

HIGHLIGHTS

● *Netherlandish Proverbs*, Bruegel
● *Portrait of Enthroned Madonna and Child*, Botticelli
● *Portrait of Georg Gisze*, Rembrandt
● *Child with Bird*, Rubens

TIP

● The air in the gallery is kept very dry to preserve the art, but you can take a break by the water sculpture *5–7–9 Series* by Walter de Maria in the central hall.

This gallery, in the Kulturforum complex, holds some 2,700 European paintings dating from the 13th to 18th centuries. Come here to see ground-breaking works by Rembrandt, Caravaggio and Bruegel.

Various collections The Gemäldegalerie collection began by bringing together various European private collections and others from royal palaces. Following World War II, the paintings were divided between East and West Berlin. In 1965, architect Rolf Gutbrod won the competition to design a complex for the museums of European art, but building work didn't start until 1985 and Gutbrod's original drawings were reworked into what is now known as the Kulturforum. After years of planning the collection was moved to the Kulturforum and opened to the public in 1998.

Rembrandt's masterpiece Moses Breaking the Tablets of the Law *(left) is just one of many important paintings on show at the Gemäldegalerie. The collection also includes works by German masters, such as this painting by Frans Hals (bottom right) as well as examples of the great Renaissance artists*

Outstanding art Dürer, Hans Holbein, Lucas Cranach the Elder and other German masters are well represented, as are the great Flemish artists Van Eyck, Rogier van der Weyden and Pieter Bruegel. Dutch baroque painting is also prominent, with several outstanding works by Rembrandt, among others. The Italian collection reads like a roll-call of great Renaissance artists: Fra Angelico, Piero della Francesco, Giovanni Bellini and Raphael. Outside, in the sculpture park, you can see works by Henry Moore and others. This large gallery is rather mazelike and, to add to the confusion, there are two room-numbering systems: Roman numerals for the larger inner rooms and standard numbers for the smaller rooms, called cabinets, on the outside. Pick up a map to help you get around and if you do get lost, return to the central hall to get your bearings.

THE BASICS

www.smb.spk-berlin.de

➕ H6

✉ Matthäikirchplatz 4–6

☎ 030 266 21 01

🕐 Tue–Wed, Fri–Sun 10–6, Thu 10–10

🍴 Cafés

🚇 U- or S-Bahn Potsdamer Platz

🚌 Bus M29, M41, 123, 148, 200

♿ Good

🎫 Moderate

Bauhaus-Archiv

The clean lines of the Bauhaus-Archiv (left) are mirrored in the designs on show (right)

THE BASICS

www.bauhaus.de

🔢 F7

✉ Klingelhöferstrasse 14

☎ 030 254 00 20

🕐 Wed–Mon 10–5

🍴 Café

🚇 U-Bahn Nollendorfplatz

🚌 Bus 100, M29, 187, 343

🚢 Bellevue

♿ Good

💶 Moderate

HIGHLIGHTS

- Walter Gropius's building
- Marcel Breuer's leather armchair
- Metal-framed furniture
- Ceramics
- Moholy-Nagy's sculpture *Light-space-modulator*
- Designs and models of Bauhaus buildings
- Paintings by Paul Klee
- Paintings by Vassily Kandinsky
- Schlemmer's theatre designs
- Marianne Brandt's tea and coffee set

Brush up on the history of design by visiting one of Berlin's foremost cultural totems—a museum celebrating the Bauhaus, one of the 20th century's most influential art and design movements.

End of decoration In the aftermath of World War I all values, artistic ones included, came under scrutiny. In Germany the dynamic outcome was the Bauhaus school, founded in 1919 by Walter Gropius in Weimar, the capital of the recently founded Republic. Gropius and his disciples stressed function, rather than decoration, preferring modern materials such as concrete and tubular steel for their versatility and appearance.

Interdisciplinary approach Mass production guaranteed the Bauhaus an unprecedented influence on European and transatlantic architecture and design. Workshops in metalwork, print and advertising, photography, painting and ceramics were coordinated by Vassily Kandinsky, Paul Klee, Oskar Schlemmer and Laszlo Moholy-Nagy.

Legacy The revolutionary credentials of the Bauhaus drove it into conflict with the Nazis. Forced to move to Dessau and then to Berlin, the school closed in 1933 but its influence lives on in the design of furniture and appliances found in many homes today.

Exhibition The display, ranging from furniture to sketches, is housed in a small museum designed by Walter Gropius in 1964.

More to See

FILMMUSEUM BERLIN (FILM MUSEUM)

A fascinating journey through the history of German film from 1895. Also includes a tribute to Marlene Dietrich.

➕ H6 ✉ Potsdamer Strasse 2 ☎ 030 30 09 030 ⏰ Tue–Sun 10–6, Thu 10–8 🚇 U- or S-Bahn Potsdamer Platz 💵 Moderate

GEDENKSTÄTTE DEUTSCHER WIDERSTAND (MEMORIAL TO GERMAN RESISTANCE)

The Bendlerblock, focus of the ill-fated conspiracy against Hitler on 20 July 1944, houses an exhibition on opposition to Hitler.

➕ G6 ✉ Stauffenbergstrasse 13 ☎ 030 26 99 50 00 ⏰ Mon–Fri 9–6, Sat, Sun 10–6 🚇 U-Bahn Kurfürstenstrasse

KUNSTGEWERBE MUSEUM

Spread out over four floors, the wide-ranging collection covers arts and crafts and interior design from the Middle Ages to the present day, with highlights from the Renaissance and postmodern periods.

➕ H6 ✉ Kulturforum, Matthaïkirchplatz ☎ 030 266 29 51 ⏰ Tue–Fri 10–6, Sat–Sun 11–6 🚇 U- or S-Bahn Potsdamer Platz

KUPFERSTICHKABINETT

The 'engravings room' is a collection of drawings and prints by some of the great European artists, including Cranach, Dürer, Pieter Bruegel the Elder, Rembrandt and Kandinsky.

➕ G6 ✉ Matthaïkirchplatz 8 ☎ 030 266 20 02 ⏰ Tue–Fri 10–6, Sat–Sun 11–6 🚇 U- or S-Bahn Potsdamer Platz 💵 Inexpensive

TOPOGRAPHIE DES TERRORS

This open-air exhibition located in the excavations of the former National Socialist government district reveals the development and activities of the National Socialist SS and Police State. The Foundation's International Documentation and Study Center, was designed by Peter Zumthor.

➕ J7 ✉ Niederkirchnerstrasse 8 ☎ 030 25 48 67 03 ⏰ May–end Sep 10–8; Apr and Oct daily 10–6 (or dusk) 🚇 U- or S-Bahn Potsdamer Platz 🚌 Bus 129, 248, 341 💵 Free

Movie buffs will love this museum that pays homage to German film history

The Scheunenviertel and Prenzlauer Berg

Experience in spirit some of Berlin's tragic past in the old Jewish Quarter and working-class district in and around Prenzlauer Berg.

DISTANCE: 4.8km (3 miles) **ALLOW:** 1.5 hours

START

ORANIENBURGER STRASSE
🚉 S-Bahn Oranienburger Strasse

END

HUSEMANNSTRASSE (▷ 91)
🚉 U-Bahn Eberswalder Strasse

❶ Start by walking eastward along Oranienburger Strasse, the heart of the Scheunenviertel (Barn Quarter). This now bustling area became the Jewish Quarter in the late 17th century.

❽ Husemannstrasse (▷ 91) now has a lively café scene, but the refurbished tenements disguise a squalid late 19th-century working-class life.

❷ Lower down, on the right, is Monbijou Park (▷ 82), once royal palace grounds, and, on the left, the remains of the Old Jewish Cemetery, destroyed by the Nazis.

❼ Cross Senefelderplatz into Kollwitzstrasse. On the right, just off Belforter Strasse, is the 19th-century water tower used by the Nazis as a makeshift torture chamber in 1933. At Kollwitzplatz (▷ 90) is a memorial to the artist Käthe Kollwitz.

❸ Turn left into Rosenthaler Strasse and then take the first left into Sophienstrasse. Between Sophienstrasse and Oranienburger Strasse are the historic courtyards known as the Hackesche Höfe (▷ 85) now smart restaurants, boutiques, art galleries and theatres.

❻ On the opposite side of Invalidenstrasse are the remains of Schinkel's Elisabethkirche (1832). Walk east along Veteranenstrasse, past the Volkspark am Weinberg and join Kastanienallee. Soon turn right into Schwedter Strasse.

❹ Continue along Sophienstrasse, passing the 18th-century Sophienkirche (▷ 83), then follow Grosse Hamburger Strasse.

❺ Cross Koppenplatz into Ackerstrasse, the heart of an old working-class quarter.

Shopping

GARAGE
Second-hand clothes are sold by weight in this large warehouse near Nollendorfplatz U-Bahn station.
➕ F7 ✉ Ahornstrasse 2 ☎ 030 211 27 60 🚇 U-Bahn Nollendorfplatz

POTSDAMER PLATZ ARKADEN
The architecturally noteworthy Renzo Piano mall has 120 shops, plus cafés and restaurants.
➕ H6 ✉ Potsdamer Platz 🚇 U- or S-Bahn Potsdamer Platz

SONY STYLE STORE
Spread out over three futuristic floors you can hear music, manipulate digital images with Sony Pictures and try out the latest Playstation.
➕ H6 ✉ Sony Center am Potsdamer Platz ☎ 030 25 75 11 55 🚇 U- or S-Bahn Potsdamer Platz

TRÖDELMARKT AM RATHAUS SCHÖNEBERG
A market that's popular with antiques dealers and tourists.
➕ Off map, south of E9 ✉ John-F-Kennedy Platz 🚇 Sat, Sun 9–4 🚇 U-Bahn Rathaus Schöneberg

Entertainment and Nightlife

CINESTAR IMAX
Berlin's biggest 3-D screen employs the latest technology and electronic glasses to bring you even closer to the action.
➕ H6 ✉ In Sony Center, Potsdamer Strasse 4 ☎ 030 26 06 64 00 🚇 U-Bahn and S-Bahn Potsdamer Platz

PHILHARMONIE
One of the world's most famous orchestras, the Berlin Philharmonic, performs in Hans Scharoun's 1960s architectural masterpiece in the Kulturforum. The acoustics are impeccable, and tickets are as rare as gold dust.
➕ H6 ✉ Herbert-von-Karajan-Strasse 1 ☎ 030 25 48 81 32 🚇 U- or S-Bahn Potsdamer Platz

SPIELBANK BERLIN
The Spielbank Berlin, the city's only even slightly Vegas-style casino, has both gambling tables and slot machines.
➕ H6 ✉ Marlene Dietrich Platz 1, at Potsdamer Platz ☎ 030 25 59 90 🕐 Daily

---
CINEMA
Going to the cinema is a popular pastime in Germany, but films are usually dubbed into German. If a film is showing in its original language version it should say OV (*Originalversion*) or OmU (*Original mit Untertiteln,* original with subtitles) on the poster outside the cinema. Hollywood blockbusters are usually released at the same time as they are elsewhere in Europe.

11.30am–6am 🚇 U- or S-Bahn Potsdamer Platz

VICTORIA BAR
A chic retro cocktail bar. An impressive list of celebrity DJs and actors drink here, attracted by the extensive classic cocktail menu and quality service.
➕ G7 ✉ Potsdamer Strasse 102 ☎ 030 25 75 99 77 🕐 Mon–Sun 6pm–3am, happy hour 6–9 🚇 U- or S-Bahn Potsdamer Platz

WINTERGARTEN VARIETE
Long synonymous with late-night entertainment, the Wintergarten makes for a fun-packed evening. International variety entertainers star.
➕ G7 ✉ Potsdamerstrasse 96 ☎ 030 250 00 88 88 🚇 U-Bahn Kurfürstenstrasse

Restaurants

PRICES

Prices are approximate, based on a 3-course meal for one person.
€€€   over €30
€€   €15–€30
€   up to €15

GLOBE (€€–€€€)

The Clarion Hotel's sophisticated restaurant covers a fair amount of culinary ground, places a strong roster on German dishes, including some local specials, along with European and other international fare.

✚ F7 ✉ Lützowplatz 17 ☎ 030 26 05 28 30 ⏰ Daily 12–10pm 🚇 U-Bahn Nollendorfplatz

GOURMETRESTAUR-ANT LORENZ FACIL (€€€)

Mediterranean cuisine with a French twist is served at the Hotel Madison's Michelin-starred restaurant. You'll be treated to first-class service in this tranquil glasshouse in a bamboo-filled quadrangle at the heart of the hotel. There is a bubbling fountain, and in summer they remove the roof to give an alfresco dining feel. Reserve ahead for this popular Zen oasis.

✚ H6 ✉ In Hotel Madison, Potsdamer Strasse 3 ☎ 030 590 05 12 34 ⏰ Mon–Fri 12–3, 7–11 🚇 S- or U-Bahn Potsdamer Platz

KAISERSAAL (€€€)

This gourmet establishment serves superior à la carte cuisine, based on the classical German-French style. Reservations are essential at this top Berlin restaurant.

✚ H6 ✉ Bellevuestrasse 1, Sony Center, Potsdamer Platz ☎ 030 2575 14 54 ⏰ Daily 7pm–12 🚇 S- and U-Bahn Potsdamer Platz

VIVO (€€€)

Chef René Conrad's adventurous cuisine and the warm-toned nature of his Mediterranean-style eatery at the Grand Hotel Esplanade has proven a worthy successor to the standout French restaurant Harlekin.

✚ F7 ✉ Lützowufer 15 ☎ 030 25 47 88 58 ⏰ Tue–Sat 6.30–11pm 🚇 U-Bahn Nollendorfplatz

Cafés

CAFÉ EINSTEIN (€€)

Traditional Viennese-style coffeehouse trying to re-create a pre-war Berlin

ANYONE FOR COFFEE?

Café culture continues to thrive in the capital. Sunday brunch is a traditional weekend pastime among Berliners and afternoon *Kaffee* and *Kuchen* (coffee and cake) is still standard practice. Traditional and independent cafés are thriving, but the American-style coffee chains are beginning to make their presence felt.

café atmosphere.

✚ F7 ✉ Kurfürstenstrasse 58 ☎ 030 261 50 96 ⏰ Daily 9am–1am 🚇 U-Bahn Nollendorfplatz

CAFÉ E GELATO (€)

Eat in or take away at this café and ice-cream shop on the top floor of the Potsdamer Platz Arkaden. Choose from an extensive selection of ice creams and sorbets—try 'Maracuja', 'Pocket Coffee' or chocolate. Alternatively, share a towering sundae or sample their cakes and generous Italian coffees, a great treat after a session of retail therapy.

✚ H6 ✉ Potsdamer Platz Arkaden Einkauf-Center ☎ 030 25 29 78 32 ⏰ Mon–Thu and Sun 10am–11pm, Fri–Sat 10am–midnight 🚇 S- and U-Bahn Potsdamer Platz

DAILY COFFEE (€)

A great way to kick-start your day is to try breakfast at this bagel and coffeehouse that opens every day early until late.

✚ H6 ✉ Friedrich-Ebert-Strasse 31 ⏰ Daily 9am–late 🚇 S-Bahn Potsdam Stadt

TIM'S CANADIAN DELI (€)

Busy café convenient to the weekend market on Winterfeldtplatz.

✚ F8 ✉ Maassenstrasse 14 ☎ 030 21 75 69 60 ⏰ Mon–Sat 8am–1am, Fri, Sun 9am–1am 🚇 U-Bahn Nollendorfplatz

Jüdisches Museum Berlin

Kreuzberg is today a multiethnic working-class community with a sizeable population of Turkish origin. It has both a vibrant—and poor—character and an increasingly gentrified face in some parts.

Bergmannstrasse

Stroll down the busy main thoroughfare to feel the pulse of this bustling part of the city

THE BASICS

✚ J9–L9
✉ Kreuzberg
🚇 U-Bahn Mehringdamm, Gneisenaustrasse, Südstern
🚌 Bus 140, 341
🍴 Many ethnic cafés and restaurants

HIGHLIGHTS

● Gneisenaustrasse
● Viktoriapark (▷ 54)
● Marheineke Markthalle
● Passionskirche
● Volkspark Heidehase

This street skirts the southern fringe of Kreuzberg and, along with Oranienstrasse (▷ 53), is one of the two defining streets of the district. It's worthwhile also taking in nearby Gneisenaustrasse.

Rainbow residents Bergmannstrasse shows the mixed face of multiethnic Kreuzberg. It's a part of the district where people from many cultural backgrounds live and work alongside each other. Two parks act like bookends to the street's course. In the west is the small Viktoriapark (▷ 54), inside which rises the low Kreuzberg hill, crowned by a military memorial in the shape of an Iron Cross. In the east is the Volkspark Heidehase, a former hunting preserve. Between these two green zones stretches Bergmannstrasse. The street's character changes quite dramatically from one side to the other. In the west it is bustling and commercial, on a small scale, lined with ethnic shops, restaurants and bars. This phase ends at about Marheinekeplatz, midway along, where market stalls selling food and clothing are clustered together under the roof of the Marheineke Markthalle.

Eastern reaches A children's playground in the square announces the start of residential east Bergmannstrasse, its southern face adjoining the grim prospect of a series of large cemeteries. In addition, there are some impressive old churches: the Passionskirche in Marheinekeplatz, the Kirche am Südstern, and the Sankt-Johannes-Basilika just around the corner in Lillienthalstrasse.

Turkish influences are evident everywhere along this important arterial route

Oranienstrasse

THE BASICS

➕ K6–M7 (and beyond)
✉ Kreuzberg
Ⓤ U-Bahn Kochstrasse, Moritzplatz, Görlitzer Bahnhof
🚌 Bus M29, 140, 256
🍴 Many ethnic cafés and restaurants

Like Bergmannstrasse (▷ 52) to the south, this long street runs roughly from west to east and is a defining axis of the Kreuzberg district. But Oranienstrasse is no twin of the other. Rather it is residential in its western reaches and bustling in its eastern.

HIGHLIGHTS

● Berlinische Galerie
● Jüdisches Museum (▷ 54)
● Moritzplatz
● Engelbeck

Turkish character In a sense Oranienstrasse has a foot in two worlds. Where it joins Kochstrasse it is virtually an extension of the city hub, with the Berlinische Galerie and the Jüdisches Museum (▷ 54) nearby. But that changes quickly to a residential area and home to the Tiyatrom, which sounds like some high-tech modern attraction but is actually the Turkish Theatre of Berlin. Appropriately enough, the farther east you go, the more pronounced Oranienstrasse's Turkish character becomes. Kreuzberg has traditionally been Berlin's alternative hub, but the trendier German elements of that character have been moving out to fast-gentrifying Prenzlauer Berg (▷ 87), leaving behind an area defined to a far greater degree by ethnic minorities, primarily Turkish.

Street traders In and around Moritzplatz, a shabby street market (▷ 55) takes place each weekend that's a good indicator of the financial difficulty some of Kreuzberg's residents endure. Farther along, Oranienplatz looks better. From here Legiendamm and Leuschnerdamm lead to the Engelbeck pond. At Oranienstrasse's eastern extremity is an enclave of decent Indian restaurants (which continues beyond the Görlitzer Bahnhof) and the famed SO 36 nightclub (▷ 55).

KREUZBERG

TOP 25

More to See

DEUTSCHES TECHNIKMUSEUM (GERMAN TECHNOLOGY MUSEUM)

A thoroughly entertaining and well-presented exhibition in the locomotive sheds of the old Anhalter train station. Everything from biplanes and vintage cars to model ships and computers. Its greatest attraction is that most of the displays are hands-on—there is even an experiment room where children can play with computers and other gadgets. Probably the most child-friendly museum in the city.

✚ H8 ✉ Trebbiner Strasse 9 ☎ 030 90 25 40 🕐 Tue–Fri 9–5.30, Sat–Sun 10–6 🚇 U-Bahn Gleisdreieck 🚌 Bus 129, 248 ♿ Moderate

JÜDISCHES MUSEUM (JEWISH MUSEUM)

This controversial building dating from 1989 by Polish-born American architect Daniel Libeskind contains an exhibition on German-Jewish history from the earliest times to the present day. A Jewish museum in Berlin has an appalling burden of history to shoulder. This fact is amplified by Libeskind's abrasive architecture (attached to an existing baroque building) and by sculptural and design elements like the installation titled *Schalechet* (Fallen Leaves, 2001), by Menashe Kadishman, which depicts more than 10,000 faces hacked out of sheet steel. But there's more than a sombre message of the Holocaust to deliver. The story of Germany's long and once rich Jewish heritage is told in an imaginative, interactive way.

✚ K7 ✉ Lindenstrasse 9–14 ☎ 030 25 99 33 00 🕐 Tue–Sun 10–8, Mon 10–10 🚇 U-Bahn Kochstrasse or Hallesches Tor ♿ Moderate

VIKTORIAPARK

Best known for Karl Friedrich Schinkel's *Monument to the Wars of Liberation* (1813–15), this park can be approached from a row of terraces and gardens. There are good views of Berlin from the summit of the park. Also has a children's playground.

✚ J9 ✉ Kreuzbergstrasse 🚇 U-Bahn Platz der Luftbrücke

Classic and modern at the Deutsches Technikmuseum (left). This Gothic-style monument stands on a hilltop in Victoria Park (right)

Shopping

BAGAGE
This shop sells bags of all shapes, sizes and colours —everything from handbags and satchels to rucksacks and travel bags.
🔹 K9 ✉ Bergmannstrasse 13 ☎ 030 693 89 16
🔘 U-Bahn Mehringdamm

BELLA CASA
A treasure trove of Middle Eastern and Oriental household furnishings and fittings, interesting ornaments, pottery, different perfumes, an array of herbs and spices and more.
🔹 K9 ✉ Bergmannstrasse 101 ☎ 030 694 07 84
🔘 U-Bahn Mehringdamm

BELLADONNA
An impressive range of natural and aromatherapy cosmetics from German companies such as Lavera, Logona, Dr. Hauschka and Weleda. Oils from Primavera.
🔹 K9 ✉ Bergmannstrasse 101 ☎ 030 694 37 31
🔘 U-Bahn Mehringdamm

BERGMANN
This friendly boutique brings all the latest men's and women's fashion labels together under one roof. A great place to find his 'n' hers fashion.
🔹 J9 ✉ Bergmannstrasse 2 ☎ 030 694 03 90
🔘 U-Bahn Mehringdamm

MORITZPLATZ FLEA MARKET
When Kreuzberg goes looking for a rock-bottom bargain, this pretensions-free fleamarket is usually where it ends up.
🔹 L7–M7 ✉ Moritzplatz
🔘 Sat–Sun 8–4 🔘 U-Bahn Moritzplatz

TÜRKISCHER MARKT
An intriguing market in the heart of the Turkish community, offering choice ethnic food—olives, cheeses and spiced chicken.
🔹 M8 ✉ Maybachufer
🔘 Tue–Fri 12–6.30
🔘 U-Bahn Schönleinstrasse

Entertainment and Nightlife

MEHRINGHOF-THEATER
Specializes in radical or alternative cabaret. Some items on the schedule are at least partly in English.
🔹 J9 ✉ Gneisenaustrasse 2a ☎ 030 691 50 99
🔘 U-Bahn Mehringdamm

POMP, DUCK AND CIRCUMSTANCE
During the four-course meal and 3½-hour show you will be treated to a bizarre ensemble of acts—not for the faint hearted.
🔹 J8 ✉ Möckernstrasse 26
☎ 030 26 94 92 00
🔘 U-Bahn Möckernbrücke

ROTE HARFE
This lively modern café is warm, welcoming and a

LANGUAGE PROBLEMS?
Even if you don't speak German, you will probably still enjoy the song and dance element of cabaret shows. However, in order to understand the political satire, some knowledge of the German language and a familiarity with current affairs is needed.

touch sophisticated. Serves an excellent weekend brunch.
🔹 Off map, east of M7
✉ Oranienstrasse 13 ☎ 030 618 44 46 🔘 Daily 10am–late
🔘 U-Bahn Görlitzer Bahnhof

SO 36
Great music from techno, Asian vibes, 1980s revival, hip-hop and house plus some bands.
🔹 M7 ✉ Oranienstrasse 190 ☎ 030 61 10 13 13 🔘 Mon from 11pm Electric Ballroom, Wed from 11pm Gay/Lesbian Party, Sun 5pm (summer 7)
🔘 U- or S-Bahn Kottbusser Tor

KREUZBERG

SHOPPING/ENTERTAINMENT AND NIGHTLIFE

Restauranti

PRICES

Prices are approximate, based on a 3-course meal for one person.

€€€ over €30
€€ €15–€30
€ up to €15

AMRIT (€€)

The warm surroundings, attentive staff, excellent food and fruity cocktails make this Indian restaurant a constant popular choice.

🚶 Off map, east of M7
✉ Oranienstrasse 202–203
☎ 030 612 55 50
🕐 Sun–Thu noon–1am, Fri and Sat noon–2am
🚇 U-Bahn Görlitzer Bahnhof

CASOLARE (€)

The staff are vocal and entertaining, particularly during an Italian football final, at this bustling trattoria. Come here for the best pizza in Berlin at the best prices. Reservations are advised at night.

🚶 M8 ✉ Grimmstrasse 30
☎ 030 69 50 66 10 🕐 Daily 12–12 🚇 U-Bahn Schönleinstrasse

HENNE (€€)

A long-time Kreuzberg institution and preferred, Henne is an old-fashioned pub-style establishment that specializes in tender roast chicken from organically raised birds, ideally washed down with a good, local beer.

🚶 M7 ✉ Leuschnerdamm 25 ☎ 030 614 77 30
🕐 Tue–Sun 7pm–1am
🚇 U-Bahn Moritzplatz

MERHABA (€–€€)

In multiethnic Kreuzberg's Werkstatt der Kulturen, one of Berlin's finest Turkish restaurants offers authentic cuisine and Anatolian ambience—along with an 'authentic' Turkish-Kreuzberg beer garden.

🚶 Off map, southeast of M9
✉ Wissmannstrasse 32
☎ 030 692 17 13
🕐 Mon–Fri 10am–11pm, Sat–Sun 12–11pm 🚇 U-Bahn Hermannplatz

OSSENA (€–€€)

Vsitors and locals alike return again and again for the warm welcome and surroundings, prompt service and excellent Italian food at affordable prices that you can expect here. For dessert, try the tiramisu—it is delicious and light.

🚶 M7 ✉ Oranienstrase 39
☎ 030 615 26 22

LITTLE ISTANBUL

Kreuzberg is a traditional working-class district near the middle of Berlin that now has the largest Turkish community outside Istanbul. In the bustling, exotic areas of Kottbusser Tor and Schlesisches Tor dozens of restaurants offer inexpensive and authentic Anatolian cuisine.

🕐 6pm–12 🚇 U-Bahn Kottbusser Tor

SUFISSIMO (€)

Come here for a meal with a more eastern flavour. Freshly prepared couscous based dishes on the menu at this café and Persian restaurant.

🚶 M9 ✉ Fichtestrasse 1
☎ 030 61 62 08 33
🕐 Sun–Fri 12–12, Sat 2pm–1am 🚇 U-Bahn Südstern

Cafés

CAFÉ AM UFER (€)

This café is a great place to be when the weather is warm. Bask in the sunshine on the terrace over a coffee or ice tea or enjoy breakfast, lunch or a light evening meal outside.

🚶 M8 ✉ Paul-Lincke-Ufer 42 ☎ 030 61 62 92 00
🕐 Daily 10am–late
🚇 U-Bahn Kottbusser Tor, Schönleinstrasse

CAFÉ ÜBERSEE (€)

Frequented by Berlin night-owls, Café Übersee is always busy with the late-night crowd into the early hours. This attractive Kreuzberg café positioned on the canal bank serves hearty breakfasts until 4pm daily.

🚶 M8 ✉ Paul-Lincke-Ufer 44 ☎ 030 618 87 65
🕐 Daily 10am–2am
🚇 U-Bahn Kottbusser Tor

Encompassing the boulevard Unter den Linden at one end and the leafy Tiergarten at the other, this district is a study in contrasts and has a wealth of historic, cultural and architectural assets.

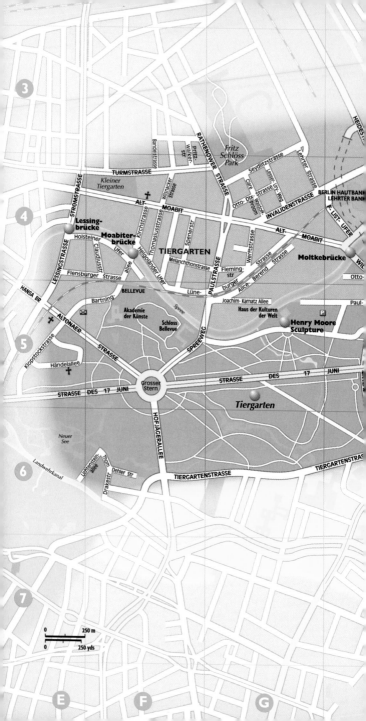

Museum für
Gegenwart

Hamburger
Bahnhof

Alexander

ufer

Philippstrasse

Luisenstrasse

Anatomisches
Theater

Oranienburger
Tor

FRIEDRICH

Schumannstrasse

Deutsches
Theater

Johannisstr

Reinhardtstr

REINHARDTSTRASSE

Albrechtstr

Friedrichstadt-
palast

Ziegelstrasse

Tucholskystrasse

STRASSE

Am Weidendamm

Kapelleufer

Marienstr

LUISENSTRASSE

Friedrich-
damm

Am Kupfergraben

Konrad
Adenauer
Str

Spree

Schiffbauer

Friedrichstrasse

Geschw
Scholl Str

von-Bismarck-
Allee

FRIEDRICHSTRASSE

Georgen-

strasse

BANDT STR

Löbe

Allee

Reichs-

tag-

ufer

Planck
Str

Universität

Maxim Gorki
Theater

Platz der
Republik

Reichstag

Dorotheen
Strasse

Jakob
Kaiser
Haus

DOROTHEENSTRASSE

Doro-

Georgstr

ferstr

SCHEIDEMANNSTRASSE

Unter den Linden

Mittelstrasse

LINDEN

Staats
Oper

Sowjetisches
Ehrenmal

UNTER

DEN

Forum
Fridericianum

Bebel-

Oper-

Brandenburger
Tor

Pariser
Platz

Komische
Oper

platz

Holocaust
Memorial

BEHRENSTRASSE

Behrenstrasse

Charlottenstrasse

Mus

BEHRENSTRASSE

Cora
Berlin
Str

WILHELMSTRASSE

FRANZÖSISCHE

STRASSE

Jägerstrasse

EBERTSTRASSE

Glinka

Mauerstrasse

FRIEDRICH

Gendarmenmarkt

Hannah Ahrendt Str

Jägerstr

Taubenstrasse

In den Min-
gärten

An der
Kolonnade

Tauben-

str

Schiller
Monument

Markgrafenstrasse

strasse

LENNÉSTRASSE

Vossstrasse

Mohren-

strasse

Stadtmitte

Mohren-

Jerus
salemer Str

Kronenstrasse

Mauer-

LEIPZIGER

STRASSE

Friedrichstrasse

Krausenstrasse

Museum für
Kommunikation

STRASSE

Charlottenstrasse

Schützenstrasse

strasse

Berlin
Hi-flyer

Zimmer-

Checkpoint
Charlie

Markgrafenstrasse

KOCHSTRASSE

Kochstrasse

H   J   K

Brandenburger Tor

Gottfried Schadow's copper sculpture tops this iconic gate

THE BASICS

➕ J5
✉ Pariser Platz
🚇 S-Bahn Unter den Linden, U-Bahn Französische Strasse
🚌 Bus 100, 147, 148, 200
♿ None
🎫 Free

HIGHLIGHTS

● *The Quadriga*
● Classical reliefs
● Adjoining classical pavilions
● View down Unter den Linden
● View down Strasse des 17. Juni
● 'Room of Silence' (in pavilion)
● Pariser Platz (▷ 64)
● Tourist office and shop

The Brandenburg Gate began life as a humble toll-gate, marking the city's western boundary. Today it symbolizes the reconciliation of East and West and is the perfect backdrop for commemorative events, celebrations and pop concerts.

Gate of peace? The gate is the work of Karl Gotthard Langhans and dates 1788–91. Its neo-classical style echoes the ancient entrance to the Acropolis in Athens, on which it is modelled. Conceived as an Arch of Peace, the Brandenburg Gate has more frequently been used to glorify martial values, as in 1933, when the Nazis' torch-light procession through the arch was intended to mark the beginning of the 1,000-year Reich.

Viktoria *The Quadriga*, a sculpture depicting the goddess Viktoria driving her chariot, was added to the gate by Johann Gottfried Schadow in 1794. In 1806, following the Prussian defeat at Jena, it was moved to Paris by Napoleon. When it was brought back in triumph less than a decade later, Karl Friedrich Schinkel added a wreath of oak leaves and the original iron cross to Viktoria's standard. During the heyday of cabaret in the 1920s, *The Quadriga* was often parodied by scantily clad chorus girls.

Pariser Platz (▷ 64) During Berlin's booming 1990s, the adjoining square was transformed. Noteworthy buildings include the Adlon Kempinski Hotel, the Academy of Arts and the DG Bank.

Friedrichstrasse

Museum Haus am Checkpoint Charlie (left, middle). The former border crossing (right)

Named for King Friedrich I of Prussia and laid out in the 18th century, elegant Friedrichstrasse bisects the central city on a north–south axis. It was itself cut in two by the East-West cleft of the Berlin Wall during the days of Berlin's division.

Street of dreams Stretching from the Oranienburger Tor to the Halleisches Tor, this is a long street, crossing the River Spree, Unter den Linden (▷ 68) and many lesser reference points on the way. Shoppers flock to Friedrichstrasse for retail therapy, or alternatively partake of the area's superior dining choices. The magic word on the street is 'bargain', if you can manage to find one in its many upmarket outlets. The flagship French chain store Galeries Lafayette (▷ 70) is just one of the stellar names. Some of the smaller streets that traverse Friedrichstrasse, such as Französische Strasse, have respectable shopping, dining and entertainment scenes of their own. Roughly midway down just off its eastern face is Gendarmenmarkt (▷ 62–63), Berlin's most handsome square and site of the impressive Konzerthaus (▷ 71).

Cold War games Friedrichstrasse was once one of the flashpoints of the East–West confrontation. The famous American Checkpoint Charlie (▷ 18) was at the lower end of Friedrichstrasse, at Zimmerstrasse. US and Red Army tanks once squared off across the brief space of that street, where tourists now snap each other's picture, but fortunately the long-barrel cannons remained cool.

THE BASICS

⊞ K7–J4
✉ Friedrichstrasse
🚇 U- and S-Bahn Friedrichstrasse; U-Bahn Oranienburger Tor, Französische Strasse, Stadtmitte, Kochstrasse and Halleisches Tor
🚌 Bus 100, 147, 148, 200, M29, M112
🍴 Many restaurants and cafés

HIGHLIGHTS

● Galeries Lafayette
● Französische Strasse
● Checkpoint Charlie (▷ 70)
● Unter den Linden (▷ 68)
● Gendarmenmarkt (▷ 62–63)

Gendarmenmarkt

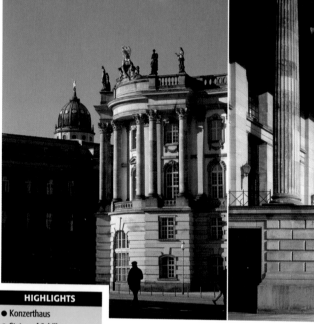

HIGHLIGHTS

- Konzerthaus
- Statue of Schiller
- Apollo in his chariot
- Deutscher Dom
- Cathedrals' twin towers

Französischer Dom
- Turmstube
- Balustrade view
- Carillon

TIP

Be sure to give yourself adequate time for the 3km (2 miles) walk, or hop on and off either public transport or the circular-tour buses.

This beautiful square comes as a pleasant surprise for visitors who associate Berlin with imperial bombast and Prussian marching bands. Climb the Französischer Dom tower for superb views of the Friedrichstadt.

Konzerthaus Known originally as the Schauspielhaus (theatre), the Konzerthaus was designed by Karl Friedrich Schinkel in 1821. Its predecessor was destroyed by fire during a rehearsal of Schiller's play *The Robbers*, so it is fitting that the playwright's monument stands outside. When the building was restored in the early 1980s after being severely damaged in World War II, the original stage and auditorium made way for a concert hall with a capacity of 1,850—hence the change of name. The façade, however, retains

This striking square of classic architecture draws crowds to the colonnaded Schauspielhaus and the fine dome of the Deutscher Dom on its far side

Schinkel's original design. Look for the sculpture of Apollo in his chariot.

Two cathedrals The twin French and German cathedrals (Französischer Dom and Deutscher Dom) occupy opposite ends of the square. The architect Karl von Gontard was described as an ass by Frederick the Great; one of the complementary cupolas collapsed in 1781. A small museum in the Deutscher Dom charts the history of German democracy from the 19th century to the present with photographs, film and a variety of objects. A museum in the Französischer Dom tells the story of the hard-working Huguenots who settled in Berlin in the 17th century, fleeing persecution in France. The Cathedral (minus its baroque tower, a later addition) was built for them.

THE BASICS

www.franzoesischer-dom-berlin.de

⊞ K5–K6

☎ Französischer Dom: 030 229 17 60. Deutscher Dom: 030 22 73 04 31

🕐 Französischer Dom: daily 9–7. Huguenot Museum: Tue–Sat 12–5, Sun 11–5. Deutscher Dom: Tue 10–10, Wed 10–7

🚇 U-Bahn Stadtmitte, Französische Strasse

🚌 Bus 147, 148

💰 Inexpensive

Pariser Platz

The square's organ grinders and ornate lamposts are reminders of a bygone age

THE BASICS

+ J5
- Pariser Platz
- Cafés and restaurants on Unter den Linden
- U-Bahn Unter den Linden
- Bus 100, 123, 200, TXL
- Free

HIGHLIGHTS

- Brandenburger Tor (▷ 60)
- Unter den Linden (▷ 68)
- Akademie der Künste
- Information boards providing history and images of the square as it was in the past

Down but not out, Berlin's once beautiful 18th-century ornamental square surrounded by palaces of the Prussian great and good, has been rebuilt along modern lines.

Risen from the Ashes Once the 'salon' of imperial Berlin, elegant Pariser Platz bit the dust entirely during World War II. With the onset of the Cold War and the construction of the Berlin Wall, which ran right next to it, the square was able to recover none of its former glory. It remained a wasteland until the reunified Berlin's booming 1990s, when the square was transformed.

New look Notable modern buildings by architects who include the American Frank O. Gehry are the Adlon Hotel, the DG Bank, the French, British and US embassies, the Akademie der Künste (Academy of the Arts) and the Dresdner Bank. A little piece of the past remains, however, in the two rectangular gardens, each one with a fountain at its heart, that occupy the square's northern and southern quadrants.

Passing pedestrians The square was once a vibrant, lively place but now has a quieter atmosphere surrounding its banks and embassies. There is, however, a constant stream of people shuffling to and fro between the Brandenburger Tor (▷ 60), which forms the square's western outlet, and the watering holes and cultural venues along Unter den Linden. The rebuilt Unter den Linden U-Bahn station adds to this just-passing-through traffic.

Size and space are awesome both inside and outside of this striking building

Reichstag

Walk up Sir Norman Foster's Dome, an impressive architectural statement, to get an inside look at the seat of the German Parliament.

Parliament building The original Reichstag was built in 1894 by Paul Wallot as the seat of the Bundestag (German Parliament). The building was damaged by fire on 27 February 1933 and was completely devastated as a result of heavy fighting around the building during World War II. After extensive restoration, the building was handed to the Federal Administration in 1973, and the first session of the reunified German Parliament was held here on 4 October 1990.

The Dome In June 1993, the British architect Sir Norman Foster was awarded the commission to restore the Reichstag. Foster preserved the original features and functions of the building, while adding glass walls, and a glass roof and chamber that bring light into the heart of the structure. Foster's Dome is visible for miles around and has a powerful presence on Berlin's skyline. It has also become a symbol of popular rule, and every day thousands of people climb to the top. Visitors are reflected in the central mirrored funnel as they walk up the gently sloping spiral walkway. From the top you can look down into the chamber, representing open democratic rule. There are information panels around the base of the funnel documenting the history of the Reichstag, and you can walk out of the Dome onto the roof terrace to appreciate the view over the city.

THE BASICS

- H5
- Platz der Republik 1
- 030 22 73 21 52
- Daily 8am–midnight
- S-Bahn Unter den Linden
- Bus 100, 123
- Free

HIGHLIGHTS

- Views of the city from Sir Norman Foster's glass dome
- View a sitting of the Bundestag from the gallery
- Black, Red and Gold (1999) artwork of German flag in west hall

Tiergarten

HIGHLIGHTS

- Zoologischer Garten
  (▷ 34)
- Kongresshalle
- Carillon
- Bismarck monument
- Schloss Bellevue
- Neuer See
- English Garden
- Soviet War Memorial

TIP

- Reaching the top of the Siegessäule is a challenge, but the view of the Tiergarten district from up there should make the climb worthwhile.

Boating, strolling, jogging, summer concerts—this huge park in the middle of Berlin offers all this and more. Look for the antique gas lamps from various European cities along the route from the station to the Landwehrkanal.

Hunting ground *Tiergarten* means 'animal garden', recalling a time when the park was stocked with wild boar and deer for the pleasure of the Prussian aristocracy. It was landscaped by Peter Joseph Lenné in the 1830s and still bears his imprint—remarkably, since the park was almost totally destroyed in World War II.

Siegessäule The Siegessäule (Victory Column) occupies a prime site on Strasse des 17. Juni, although it originally stood in front of the

Berlin's green lung, the Tiergarten, provides an essential space for city dwellers to relax. The Siegessäule victory column (far left and detail, far right) bears scars from gunfire during World War II

Reichstag. Erected in 1873 to commemorate Prussian victories against Denmark, Austria and France, the 67m (220ft) column is decorated with captured cannon. 'Gold Else', the victory goddess on the summit, beloved by Berliners, is waving her laurel wreath wryly towards Paris.

War heroes and revolutionaries The three heroes of the Wars of Unification—Count Otto von Bismarck and Generals Helmut von Moltke and Albrecht von Roon—are fêted with statues to the north of the Siegessäule. Memorials to two prominent revolutionaries, Karl Liebknecht and Rosa Luxemburg, stand beside the Landwehrkanal near Lichtensteinallee. Their bodies were dumped in the canal in 1919 by members of the right-wing Free Corps who had shot them shortly after an abortive Communist uprising.

THE BASICS

Siegessäule

➕ F5

✉ Grosser Stern, Strasse des 17. Juni

☎ 030 391 29 61

🕐 Mon–Thu 9.30–6.30, Fri–Sun 9.30–7

🚇 S-Bahn Tiergarten

🚌 Bus 100, 187, 343

♿ None

💶 Inexpensive

❓ Viewing platform (no elevator)

Unter den Linden

The classically styled Opera House (right) presides over eastern Unter den Linden (left)

The street 'Under the Linden Trees', once the heart of imperial Berlin, has fine neo-classical and baroque buildings. The pièce de résistance is Andreas Schlüter's superb sculptures of dying warriors in the courtyard of the Zeughaus.

Forum Fridericianum Frederick the Great presides over the eastern end of Unter den Linden. His equestrian statue, by Daniel Christian Rauch, stands next to Bebelplatz, once known as the Forum Fridericianum and intended to evoke the grandeur of Imperial Rome. Dominating the square is Georg von Knobelsdorff's opera house, the Deutsche Staatsoper (▷ 71). Facing it is the Old Royal Library (Alte-Königliche Bibliothek), completed in 1780. Here, in 1933, Nazi propaganda chief Josef Goebbels consigned the works of ideological opponents to the flames in a public book-burning. Just south of Bebelplatz is the Roman Catholic cathedral, the Hedwigskirche, whose classical lines echo the Pantheon in Rome.

Zeughaus Frederick's civic project was never completed, but the buildings on the opposite side of Unter den Linden keep up imperial appearances. The Humboldt University was designed by Johann Boumann as a palace for Frederick the Great's brother in 1748. Next comes the Neue Wache (Guardhouse), designed by Schinkel in 1818 to complement Johann Nering's 1695 baroque palace, the Zeughaus (Arsenal). The Deutsches Historisches Museum (German History Museum) is in the Zeughaus.

BERLIN HI-FLYER
A huge, secured helium balloon rises up to a height of 150m (492ft).
➕ J6 ✉ Corner of Wilhelmstrasse and Zimmerstrasse ☎ 030 226 67 88 11 ⏰ Summer: Sun–Thu 10–10, Fri–Sat 10am–12.30am; winter: Sun–Thu 11–6, Fri–Sat 11–7 🚇 S- and U-Bahn Mohrenstrasse 🚌 Bus M24, M41, 123, 148, 200, 348, TXL 💷 Expensive

DENKMAL FÜR DIE ERMORDETEN JUDEN EUROPAS (MEMORIAL FOR THE MURDERED JEWS OF EUROPE)
This striking memorial is a field of *stelae*, through which you can stroll.
➕ J5 ✉ Between Ebertstrasse and Wilhelmstrasse ☎ 030 26 39 43 11 ⏰ Memorial permanently; Information Centre daily 10–8 🚇 U-Bahn Unter den Linden 🚌 Bus 123, 200 💷 Free

HENRY MOORE SCULPTURE, HAUS DER KULTUREN DER WELT
Henry Moore's statue, *Large Butterfly* (1984), 'flutters' over a lake outside the Kongresshalle.

➕ G5 ✉ John-Foster-Dulles-Allee 🚇 S-Bahn Unter den Linden

LESSINGBRÜCKE
Scenes from playwright Gotthold Ephraim Lessing (1729–81) dramas decorate the piers of 'his' bridge.
➕ E4 ✉ Lessingstrasse 🚇 U-Bahn Turmstrasse

MOABITER BRÜCKE
This bridge of 1864 is famous for the four bears that decorate it.
➕ F4 ✉ Bellevue Ufer 🚇 S-Bahn Bellevue

MOLTKEBRÜCKE
Named for a hero of the Franco-Prussian war, this bridge is guarded by Prussian armed eagles and cherubs.
➕ H4 ✉ Willi-Brandt-Strasse 🚇 S-Bahn Lehrter Bahnhof

SCHILLER MONUMENT
In the Gendarmenmarkt (▷ 62–63) is Reinhold Begas' monument to Schiller (1869).
➕ K6 ✉ Gendarmenmarkt 🚇 U-Bahn Stadtmitte, Französische Strasse

The Berlin Hi-Flyer (right)

Looking down the river Spree-Bellvue to Lessing Bridge (left)

Shopping

BERLE'S TRENDS AND GIFTS

A great place for purchasing designer-ish personal and household gifts, for both adults and children, especially if you are not a fan of traditional souvenirs.

🚹 K6 ✉ Mohrenstrasse 50 ☎ 030 20 67 39 30 🔵 U-Bahn Stadtmitte

BERLINER ANTIK UND FLOHMARKT

Affordable antiques and bric-à-brac beneath the arches of Friedrichstrasse station.

🚹 J5 ✉ Georgenstrasse ⏰ Wed–Mon 11–6 🔵 U- or S-Bahn Friedrichstrasse

BERLINER KUNST-UND-NOSTALGIE-MARKT

Art and nostalgia—or the most part paintings, drawings and antiques.

🚹 K4–K5 ✉ Am Kupfergraben 🔵 U- or S-Bahn Friedrichstrasse

BÜRGEL-HAUS

Blue-and-cream pottery from the German region of Thüringia at very reasonable prices.

🚹 J5 ✉ Friedrichstrasse 154 ☎ 030 204 45 19 🔵 U-Bahn Französische Strasse

DOM

Add a touch of sparkle to your home with kitsch accessories and lamps or treat a friend to one of the innovative gifts from this shop.

🚹 K5 ✉ Friedrichstrasse 76

☎ 030 20 94 73 95 🔵 U-Bahn Französische Strasse

DUSSMANN: DAS KULTURHAUS

This huge book and record store is ideal for last-minute present buying. Where CDs are concerned, if they don't have it here, you won't find it anywhere. Stays open until 10pm.

🚹 K5 ✉ Friedrichstrasse 90 ☎ 030 20 25 20 59 🔵 U- or S-Bahn Friedrichstrasse

FASSBENDER & RAUSCH

A luxury chocolate shop and confectioner founded in the 19th century which still sells all manner of delicious goodies for chocaholics.

🚹 K6 ✉ Charlottenstrasse 60 ☎ 030 20 45 84 40 🔵 U-Bahn Stadtmitte

---

FRIEDRICHSTRASSE

Rebuilt almost from scratch during the last decade, Friedrichstrasse is rapidly becoming a magnet for discerning shoppers, especially aficionados of the latest designer fashions. Galeries Lafayette (see this page), also here, is the first branch of the famous department store outside France. Apart from Jean Nouvel's highly innovative open-plan design, the main talking point is the mouth-watering Food Hall, selling everything from pâtés to oysters.

FRIEDRICHSTADT-PASSAGEN Q205

Some 50 de luxe shops and boutiques occupy this elegant shopping mall, along with several chic restaurants and cafés.

🚹 K6 ✉ Friedrichstrasse 67 ☎ 030 2094 51 01 🔵 U-Bahn Stadtmitte

GALERIES LAFAYETTE

Branch of the Parisian shopping mecca (see panel). An architectural treat, too, with its impressive curved glass wall, curved roof and two glass cones inside.

🚹 K5 ✉ Friedrichstrasse 78 ☎ 030 20 94 80 ⏰ Mon–Sat 10–8 🔵 U-Bahn Französische Strasse

HAUS AM CHECK-POINT CHARLIE

The only place in Berlin where you can still find an authentic piece of the Wall; also GDR and Soviet Union medals, military insignia and much more.

🚹 K6 ✉ Friedrichstrasse 43–45 ☎ 030 253 72 50 🔵 U-Bahn Kochstrasse

MEISSENER PORZELLAN

For lovers of fine china, Meissener Porzellan sells figurines and other decorative items made from the famous—and expensive—handmade Meissen porcelain.

🚹 J5 ✉ Unter den Linden 39B ☎ 030 22 67 90 28 🔵 U-Bahn Unter den Linden

Entertainment and Nightlife

BERLINER ENSEMBLE
Playwright Bertolt Brecht founded this famous theatre company in 1948. His plays are still in the repertoire.
➕ J4 ✉ Bertolt-Brecht-Platz ☎ 030 282 31 60 Ⓜ U-or S-Bahn Friedrichstrasse

DEUTSCHE STAATSOPER
The best of both home-grown and international opera and ballet are performed in a beautiful baroque concert hall.
➕ J5 ✉ Unter den Linden 7 ☎ 030 20 35 40 Ⓜ U-Bahn Hausvogteiplatz

DEUTSCHES THEATER
The name of theatre director Max Reinhardt was virtually synonymous with the life of this theatre from the turn of the 20th the century until the Nazis came to power. Film star Marlene Dietrich performed here.
➕ J4 ✉ Schumannstrasse 13 ☎ 030 28 44 12 21 Ⓜ U- or S-Bahn Friedrichstrasse

DISTEL
'The Thistle' club is known for its acerbic political satire.
➕ K4 ✉ Friedrichstrasse 101 ☎ 030 204 47 04 Ⓜ U- or S-Bahn Friedrichstrasse

FRIEDRICHSTADT-PALAST
The most famous nightspot in eastern Berlin, with a long tradition. In the main revue entertainment includes variety acts, a floor show and loud music; the small revue is more intimate.
➕ J4 ✉ Friedrichstrasse 107 ☎ 030 23 26 22 03 Ⓜ U- or S-Bahn Friedrichstrasse

HAUS DER KULTUREN DER WELT
This modern multicultural foundation in the Tiergarten regularly hosts rock concerts and showcases African and Latin American music.
➕ G5 ✉ John-Foster-Dulles-Allee 10 ☎ 030 39 78 70 Ⓜ S-Bahn Unter den Linden

KOMISCHE OPER BERLIN
Modern and inventive productions of opera, dance and musical theatre.
➕ J5 ✉ Behrenstrasse 55–57 ☎ 030 47 99 74 00 Ⓜ U-Bahn Französische Strasse

---

DEUTSCHE STAATSOPER
The handsome neoclassical building dominating Bebelplatz is Berlin's oldest opera house, the Deutsche Staatsoper (see this page), built in the reign of Frederick the Great. It is currently engaged in a struggle with the Deutsche Oper (▷ 27), for government subsidies. Musicians who have graced this stage include the composers Mendelssohn, Meyerbeer, Liszt and Richard Strauss and conductor Wilhelm Furtwängler.

MAXIM GORKI THEATER
This theatre stages plays by contemporary dramatists and works by classical German playwrights. The Gorki Studio has an experimental playlist.
➕ K5 ✉ Am Festungsgraben 2 ☎ 030 20 22 11 29 Ⓜ U- or S-Bahn Friedrichstrasse

NEWTON BAR
Designer good looks extend from the racy Helmut Newton posters to the black leather armchairs—and to the cocktail-sipping clientele. Cigar fanciers can enjoy a Cuban smoke in the separate cigar lounge.
➕ K5 ✉ Am Festungsgraben 2 ☎ 030 20 22 11 29 Ⓜ U- or S-Bahn Friedrichstrasse

SCHAUSPIELHAUS BERLIN (KONZERTHAUS)
The magnificent concert hall of the Berlin Symphony Orchestra was designed by architect Karl Friedrich Schinkel in 1818.
➕ K5 ✉ Gendarmenmarkt 2 ☎ 030 203 09 21 01 Ⓜ U-Bahn Französische Strasse

TRÄNENPALAST
The 'Palace of Tears', the former hall for border and customs procedures is now a concert venue for rock and pop concerts, discos and cabaret.
➕ J5 ✉ Reichstagufer 17 ☎ 030 206 10 00 Ⓜ U- or S-Bahn Friedrichstrasse

Restaurants

BOCCA DI BACCO (€€€)

This is the place to go for gourmet Italian food. The food is posh and the address exclusive, and the staff are friendly and welcoming.

⊞ K5 ⊠ Friedrichstrasse 167–168 ☎ 030 20 67 28 28 ⊙ Mon–Sat 12–11.30, Sun 6pm–11.30pm ⊕ U- or S-Bahn Friedrichstrasse

BORCHARDT (€€€)

With historical roots going back to 1853, this fine French restaurant is one of the most venerable dining establishments in town, though its interior design is more 1920s than 19th century Berlin.

⊞ K5 ⊠ Französische Strasse 47 ☎ 030 81 88 62 62 ⊙ Daily 12–12 ⊕ U-Bahn Französische Strasse

DRESSLER (€€)

Aims to re-create the classic dining style of 1920s and 1930s Berlin in a bustling ambience where waiters in aprons serve everything from coffee to venison (a sister eatery is on Kurfürstendamm).

⊞ J5 ⊠ Unter den Linden 39 ☎ 030 204 44 22 ⊙ Daily 8am–1am ⊕ S-Bahn Unter den Linden

CAFÉ DE FRANCE (€€)

The food is traditionally French but the look of the restaurant and the furnishings are modern at this popular bistro.

⊞ J5 ⊠ Unter den Linden 62–68 ☎ 030 20 64 13 91 ⊙ Mon–Sat 10–10, Sun 10–6 ⊕ S-Bahn Unter den Linden

LUTTER & WEGNER (€€€)

This historic 19th-century restaurant on the Gendarmenmarkt has Austrian as well as German cuisine; also a wine bar.

⊞ K6 ⊠ Charlottenstrasse 56 ☎ 030 20 29 54 10 ⊙ Daily 11am–3am ⊕ U-Bahn Französische Strasse

MARGAUX (€€€)

Fine dining at its best. Expect a few avant-garde creations and some classic à la carte dishes at this 1 Michelin star first-rate restaurant.

⊞ J5 ⊠ Unter den Linden 78 ☎ 030 22 65 26 11 ⊙ Mon–Fri 7pm–10.30pm ⊕ S-Bahn Unter den Linden

OPERNPALAIS UNTER DEN LINDEN CAFÉ (€)

Redolent of old Berlin, this palatial café with an expensive restaurant upstairs is next to the Staatsoper.

⊞ K5 ⊠ Unter den Linden 5 ☎ 030 20 26 83 ⊙ Daily 8am–midnight ⊕ U-Bahn Französische Strasse

VAU (€€€)

Vau is one of the best restaurants in the city. Come here for a menu of updated German-Austrian cuisine.

⊞ K5 ⊠ Jägerstrasse 54–55 ☎ 030 202 97 30 ⊙ Mon–Sat 12–2.30, 7–10.30 ⊕ U-Bahn Französische Strasse

DIE ZWÖLF APOSTEL (€–€€)

Red velvet curtains, candlelight, painted ceilings and an open kitchen with fresh ingredients all add to the theatrical experience. All pizzas are reduced 12–4.

⊞ K5 ⊠ Georgenstrasse 2 ☎ 030 201 02 22 ⊙ Mon–Thu 11am–midnight, Fri–Sat 11am–1am ⊕ U- and S-Bahn Friedrichstrasse

Many of Germany's premier museums are clustered near Alexanderplatz, on the Museumsinsel. But this core of the former East Berlin, beside the River Spree, has far more to offer than just museum-hopping.

Linien- strasse
Gr. Hambu..
Auguststrasse
Neue Synagoge
ORANIENBURGER
Krausnickstr
STRASSE
Ziegelstrasse
Monbijou Park
Pergamon Museum
Nation. Galeri
Am Kupfergraben
Museumsinsel
Bodestr
Ägyptisches Museum
Deut Hist Mus
Schlossbrück
Friedrich-werdersche Kirche
WERDER
P
LEIPZIGER
Krausenstrass
Schützenstrass
Zimmerstrass
KOCHSTRASSE
P
Junkerstr
Fei..

0 250 m
0 250 yds

3
4
5
6
7

H   J   K

Alexanderplatz

The TV tower (left). The World Clock (centre) and trams (right) feature in the square

A victim of East German town planning, 'Alex' (as Berliners affectionately call this historic old market place) is waiting to be revamped by a new generation of architects with a mandate to return it to the people.

Historic square Alexanderplatz is named after Russian Tsar Alexander I, who once reviewed troops here. The square was colonized by Berlin's burgeoning working class in the middle of the 19th century. Crime flourished, so it is no accident that the police headquarters was nearby.

TV tower The Fernsehturm rises like an unlovely flower from the middle of the square. Its single virtue is its great height, which at 362m (1,188ft) exceeds even that of Paris's Eiffel Tower. Climb it on a fine day for panoramic city views. The cost of Hans Koplhoff's ambitious plans for the eventual development of the square may be prohibitive.

Other attractions In the square's southwestern quadrant, the spectacular Neptunbrunnen (Neptune Fountain), which was a gift to Kaiser Wilhelm II in 1891, stood originally in Schlossplatz. Its focal point is a massive bronze sculpture of the Roman god of the sea. Around the fountain's rim sit female statues representing the rivers Rhine, Oder, Elbe and Weichsel. The Marienkirche has a 15th-century nave and a lantern tower added by Karl Gotthard Langhans in 1790. An epidemic of the plague in 1484 is commemorated in a large medieval wall painting *Totentanz* (*Dance of Death*).

The ornate decoration (left), and the imposing exterior, of the Berliner Dom (right)

Berliner Dom

For evidence of imperial pretensions, look to Berlin's Protestant cathedral. The cathedral's vast vault contains the sarcophagi of more than 90 members of the Hohenzollern dynasty.

Cathedral Architect Julius Raschdorff built the Berliner Dom over the site of a smaller imperial chapel. The existing cathedral was completed in 1905 and opened in the presence of Kaiser Wilhelm II. Inside, the most impressive feature is the dome that is 74m (234ft) high, supported by pillars of Silesian sandstone and decorated with mosaics of the Beatitudes by Anton von Werner. In High Renaissance style, the dome, open to the public and reached by climbing 270 steps, is reminiscent of St. Peter's in Rome. The cathedral was badly damaged during World War II, but restoration started in 1974 after years of neglect and is now well advanced. Work on the stained-glass windows has been completed.

Destroyed by Allied bombs The name of the square, Lustgarten, derives from the former pleasure garden, which stood just outside the cathedral on Museumsinsel. The site, where the Great Elector is said to have planted potatoes, is now covered by grass and paving. Opposite, until the Allied bombings in World War II, stood the enormous Berliner Schloss, dating from the early 18th century and designed by Andreas Schlüter and Johann Eosander von Goethe. The statue of the Great Elector, now in front of Schloss Charlottenburg, once stood here.

THE BASICS

➕ L5
✉ Am Lustgarten
☎ 030 20 26 91 90
🕐 Apr–end Sep Mon–Sat 9–8, Sun 12–8; Oct–end Mar Mon–Sat 9–8, Sun 12–7
🍽 None
Ⓤ U- and S-Bahn Alexanderplatz, S-Bahn Hackescher Markt
🚌 Bus 100, 148, 348
♿ Few
✋ Moderate

HIGHLIGHTS

● Lustgarten
● High Renaissance–style façade
● Baptism chapel
● Imperial staircase
● Sarcophagi
● Dome 74m (234ft) high
● Figures above altar
● Viewing gallery

ALEXANDERPLATZ

★

TOP 25

HIGHLIGHTS

● View of Altes Museum from the Lustgarten
● Rotunda of Altes Museum
● *Unter den Linden*, Franz Krüger (Alte Nationalgalerie)
● *Portrait of Frederick the Great at Potsdam*, Adolph Menzel (Alte Nationalgalerie)
● View from Monbijou Bridge

TIP

● You may be tempted to 'do' the Museumsinsel in one go. The museums are close together but each one is worth a half-day visit at least.

Berlin's famed collection of antiquities is one of the city's major treasures. To see it, head for Museums Island, accessible over the Monbijou Bridge, on the Spree. The Pergamon (▷ 81) is one of five superb institutions there.

Altes Museum Built in 1830, this was the first museum on the island. Karl Schinkel's magnificent classical temple shares with the Pergamon (▷ 81) fabulous collections of sculptures, paintings and objects from all corners of the ancient world. The impression made by the façade is overwhelming, and hidden at the core of the building is a rotunda inspired by Rome's Pantheon and lined with statues of the gods.

Neues Museum From 2009 Berlin's famed Egyptian collections will be housed once again in this museum, designed in 1843 by August Stüler.

Ancient history in a modern city—the Altes Museum (left, top middle, bottom right and far right bottom) has a fascinating collection of antiquities from around the world. Highlight of the Egyptian Museum is the bust of Queen Nefertiti (top right). Berlin's National Gallery on Museumsinsel (bottom middle)

Bode-Museum Named after Wilhelm von Bode (1845–1929), for 20 years curator of Museums Island, this 1904 building will exhibit exquisite medieval sculptures, early Christian and Byzantine art. Scheduled to reopen at the end of 2006.

Alte Nationalgalerie This gallery displays mainly paintings of the 19th century, and includes works by Impressionists such as Manet, Monet and Degas.

Ägyptisches Museum (Egyptian Museum) This rich collection of 2,000 ancient masterpieces spans three millennia. The highlight here is the bust of Queen Nefertiti, wife of Pharaoh Akhenaton. Dating from about 1340BC, the bust, made of limestone and plaster, was discovered in 1912 along with other royal portraits. Another highlight is the Temple Gate of Kalabsha, built by the Roman Emperor Augustus in 20BC. Other exhibits include Roman mummy masks, jewellery and games.

THE BASICS

www.smb.museum.de
⊞ K4, K5, L5
✉ Museumsinsel
☎ 030 20 90 55 77 (info)
🕐 While rebuilding continues, some museums are open only for temporary exhibitions Tue–Sun 10–6
🚇 S-Bahn Hackescher Markt, U- and S-Bahn Friedrichstrasse
🚌 Bus 100, 157, 200,TXL
♿ Few
💷 Moderate

Nikolaiviertel

TOP **25**

Bronze statues (left) and period houses complement this medieval-style area

THE BASICS

www.stadtmuseum.de

🔲 L5

✉ Poststrasse

☎ Nikolaikirche: 03 24 72 45 29. Knoblauchhaus: 030 23 45 99 91. Ephraim-Palais: 030 24 00 21 21

🕓 Knoblauchhaus, Ephraim-Palais and Nikolaikirche: Tue–Sun 10–6, Wed noon–8

🚇 U- and S-Bahn Alexanderplatz

🚌 Bus 100, 147, 148, 200, TXL

♿ Few

🎟 All: moderate

HIGHLIGHTS

Nikolaikirche
● Exhibition of Berlin history
● Gothic nave
● *The Good Samaritan*, Michael Ribestein
● Hunger Cloth (in vestry)
● Wooden *Crucifixion* of 1485

Enjoy a wander through the Nikolai Quarter, a diverting pastiche of baroque and neoclassical architecture, with rows of gabled houses, cobbled streets and quaint shops.

Nikolaikirche The dominating landmark is the twin-spire church that gives the Nikolaiviertel its name. The Nikolaikirche is the oldest church in Berlin, dating originally from 1200 although the present building was not completed until 1470. Seriously damaged in World War II, the beautifully proportioned Gothic nave has been sensitively restored. The church is of great historic importance, because it was here, in 1307, that the two communities of Berlin and Cölln were formally united. The church, now used for services only occasionally, houses a museum of Berlin history.

Around the Quarter Two other notable buildings recall the lavish lifestyle of Imperial Berlin. The pink stuccoed Knoblauchhaus was designed in 1759 by Friedrich Wilhelm Dietrichs for one of Berlin's most distinguished families. The extravagant Ephraim-Palais, with golden balconies and stone cherubs, belonged to Frederick the Great's banker, Nathan Ephraim. The interior is decorated with art of the 17th to the 19th centuries.

Most picturesque Among streets, the title probably goes to Eiergasse and Am Nussbaum, named for its cheery reconstruction of a famous 16th-century Berlin inn, Zum Nussbaum (▷ 86) ('At the Nut Tree')—a good refreshment stop.

The Pergamon Altar (left). Wall design in the Aleppo Room (centre). The Ishtar Gate (right)

If you have time to visit only one museum in Berlin, choose the Pergamon. Virtually every corner of the ancient world is represented, from the Roman Empire to the Islamic world.

Controversy Like the other museums on Museums Island (Museumsinsel ▷ 78–79), the Pergamon was built to house the vast haul of antiquities amassed by German archaeologists in the 19th century. Controversy rages over the proper home for such relics; some people argue that they were wrongfully plundered. Restoration of the museum is due to begin in 2008.

Pergamon Altar The museum's most stunning exhibit is the famous Pergamon Altar from Asia Minor, a stupendous monument so huge that it needs a hall more than 15m (50ft) high to accommodate it. From Bergama on the west coast of Turkey, it was excavated by Carl Humann in 1878–86. Dating from about 164BC, it was part of a complex of royal palaces, temples, a library and a theatre. Hardly less impressive is the reconstructed market gateway of Miletus, built by the Romans in this town in western Turkey in AD120 during the reign of Emperor Hadrian.

Antiquities The museum also has a splendid collection of Greek and Roman statues (some of them retaining traces of their original vibrant tones), Islamic art, figurines and clay tablets. Many more objects come from Sumeria and other parts of the Middle East.

THE BASICS

www.smpk.de
🔲 K4
✉ Am Kupfergraben, Museumsinsel
☎ 030 20 90 55 57 (info)
🕐 Tue–Sun 10–6. (Thu 10–10)
🍴 Café
🚆 S-Bahn Hackescher Markt
🚌 Bus 100, 147, 200, TXL
♿ Few
💲 Moderate

HIGHLIGHTS

● 120m (394ft) frieze on Pergamon Altar
● Market gate from Miletus
● Ishtar Gate
● Façade of Mshatta Palace
● Nebuchadnezzar's throne room
● Figurines from Jericho
● Panel room from Aleppo
● Bust of the Emperor Caracalla
● Statue of Aphrodite from Myrina

More to See

FRIEDRICHSBRÜCKE

This elegant bridge, built in 1892, provides a fine view of the Berliner Dom.
➕ L4–L5 ✉ Bodestrasse 🚇 S-Bahn Hackescher Markt

FRIEDRICHWERDERSCHE KIRCHE

Berlin's celebrated architect Karl Friedrich Schinkel designed this church in neo-Gothic style in 1824. It is now a museum as a tribute to his work.
➕ K5 ✉ Werderscher Markt ☎ 030 208 13 23 🕐 Tue–Sun 10–6 🚇 U-Bahn Hausvogteiplatz 🖐 Free

GERTRAUDENBRÜCKE

Gertraud was a preferred saint of the fisherfolk who used to ply the waters here in the Middle Ages. Bronze water rats decorate the base of her statue.
➕ L6 ✉ Gertraudenstrasse 🚇 U-Bahn Spittelmarkt

JUNGFERNBRÜCKE

This drawbridge, dating from 1798, was once the haunt of Huguenot girls selling silk and lace.

➕ L5 ✉ Friedrichsgracht 🚇 U-Bahn Spittelmarkt

MÄRKISCHES MUSEUM

A visit here is a stroll back down Berlin's memory lane, from the foundation of the city in the 13th-century, through its rise to be Prussian and then German capital, the Nazi period, Cold War division, and reunification.
➕ M6 ✉ Am Köllnischen Park 5 ☎ 030 30 86 62 15 🕐 Tue and Thu–Sun 10–6, Wed 12–8pm 🚇 Märkisches Museum 🖐 Moderate

MARX AND ENGELS

The two founders of Communism stand forlorn in a tawdry garden near Alexanderplatz.
➕ L5 ✉ Rathausstrasse 🚇 U-Bahn Alexanderplatz

MONBIJOU PARK

This park, near Museums Island, has a playground and a splash pool for toddlers.
➕ K4 ✉ Oranienburger Strasse 🚇 S-Bahn Hackescher Markt

Marx and Engels Monument, Rathaustrasse

Neoclassical sculptures in Friedrichwerdersche Kirche

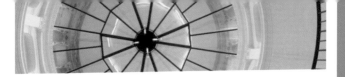

NEUE SYNAGOGE (NEW SYNAGOGUE)

The stunning dome of this 1866 building is one of Berlin's landmarks. Designed by Eduard Knoblauch and August Stüler, it was destroyed during World War II. Rebuilding finished in 1995.

🔲 K4 ✉ Oranienburger Strasse 28–30 ☎ 030 88 02 83 00 🕓 Sun–Thu 10–5.30, Fri 10–1.30 🚇 S-Bahn Oranienburger Strasse

ROTES RATHAUS

Designed by Heinrich Friedrich Waesemann who was inspired by the architecture of Renaissance Italy, the Berliner Rathaus (Town Hall) is known as the Rotes (Red) Rathaus on account of its colour.

🔲 L5 ✉ Rathausstrasse 5 ☎ 030 902 6 0 🕓 Mon–Fri 9–6 🚇 U- and S-Bahn Alexanderplatz 🖐 Free

SEA LIFE CENTER BERLIN

Take a ride through the middle of this cylindrical domed aquarium in a glass elevator and travel into an underwater world full of tropical fish.

L5 ✉ Spandauer Strasse 3 ☎ 030 99 28 00 🕓 Sep–end Mar daily 10–6; Apr–end Oct daily 10–7 🚇 S-Bahn Hackescher Markt 🚌 Bus 100, 148, 200, TXL 🖐 Expensive

SCHLEUSENBRÜCKE

This simple iron bridge is decorated with historic scenes of Berlin.

🔲 K5 ✉ Werderstrasse 🚇 U-Bahn Hausvogteiplatz

SCHLOSSBRÜCKE

Karl Friedrich Schinkel designed a new bridge to replace the decrepit Hundebrücke in 1819. Named after a royal palace that no longer exists, it is decorated with statues of Greek gods.

🔲 K5 ✉ Unter den Linden 🚇 U-Bahn Hausvogteiplatz

SOPHIENKIRCHE

Berlin's sole surviving baroque church, completed in 1734, was designed by J. F. Grael.

🔲 L4 ✉ Grosse Hamburger Strasse 29 ☎ 030 308 79 20 🕓 May–end Oct Wed 3–6, Sun 10 (service) 🚇 U-Bahn Weinmeisterstrasse

★

Schlossbrücke, or Palace Bridge, is located between the Palace Square and the avenue Unter den Linden (left); bridge marble sculpture detail (right)

Berlin Mitte

A stroll through a part of town that was the heart of the former East Berlin.

DISTANCE: 4.4km (2.75 miles) **ALLOW:** 1.5 hours

START

BRANDENBURGER TOR (▷ 60)
⬛ J5 🚇 S-Bahn Unter den Linden

END

BRANDENBURGER TOR (▷ 60)
⬛ J5 🚇 S-Bahn Unter den Linden

1 Walk down the left-hand side of Unter den Linden (▷ 68) with your back to Pariser Platz and the Brandenburg Gate. After 150m (165 yards), pass Hotel Adlon Kempinski (▷ 68) on your right.

2 Cross Neustädtische Kirch-strasse. Cross Hinter dem Griefhaus, passing the Zeughaus (▷ 68) (Arsenal) on the left, now the Deutsches Historisches Museum.

3 Unter den Linden becomes Schinkelallee, which takes you over the River Spree. Continue ahead, keeping Museums Island (▷ 78) and the Berliner Dom (▷ 77) on the left. Go over the Liebknecht bridge, cross the road to Marx-Engels-Forum.

4 Walk to the Nikolaikirche (▷ 80). Turn right onto Propstrasse and walk west. Continue to the River Spree, turn right down Spree Ufer towards the Berliner Dom. Turn left onto Rathausstrasse and cross the bridge.

7 From the Schinkel monument, leave the square between the Schauspielhaus (Playhouse) and the Französischer Dom. Go right on to Charlottenstrasse. Cross the road and continue to rejoin Französische Strasse, turn left. At the traffic lights turn right into Friedrichstrasse (▷ 61), go back to Unter den Linden and the Brandenburg Gate.

6 Head back onto Werderstrasse on the right; this becomes Französische Strasse. Soon turn left into Mark-grafenstrasse and cross over into Gendarmenmarkt (▷ 62).

5 Walk west towards the redbrick twin towers of the Friedrichswerder-sche Kirche (▷ 82), crossing Breite Strasse. Walk along Werderscher Markt.

Shopping

FACHHANDELS-GESCHÄFT RASCHKE

Traditional wooden, beautifully crafted handmade Christmas decorations.
🔲 L4 ✉ Neuer Hackescher Markt, Dircksenstrasse 50 ☎ 030 28 38 80 10 🚇 S-Bahn Hackescher Markt

G-STAR STORE

Stylish designer denim for men and women at this Dutch store in the heart of the city.
🔲 K4 ✉ Oranienburger Strasse 12 ☎ 030 24 63 25 54 🚇 S-Bahn Hackescher Markt

HACKESCHE HÖFE

Now smartened up and commericalized, these historic courtyards remain at the forefront of Berlin's contemporary art scene with art galleries, workshops and cafés.
🔲 L4 ✉ Rosenthaler Strasse 40–41 ☎ No phone 🚇 S-Bahn Hackescher Markt

KUNST-WERKE BERLIN

Experimental and avantgarde art. This is one of Auguststrasse's new galleries.
🔲 K4 ✉ Auguststrasse 69 ☎ 030 243 45 90 🚇 S-Bahn Oranienburger Strasse

NIX MODE-DESIGN

Sophisticated fashion sold here includes chic clothing for men, women and children. The shop is in Mitte.
🔲 K4 ✉ Oranienburger Strasse 32, Heckmann Höfe ☎ 030 281 80 44 🚇 S-Bahn Oranienburger Strasse

STERLING GOLD

This shop in Mitte has an good range of glamorous evening, ball and cocktail wear from the 1950s to the 1980s. The shop has its own dressmaker who can transform any dress into a perfect fit.
🔲 L3 ✉ Heckmann Höfe ☎ 030 28 09 65 00 🚇 S-Bahn Oranienburger Strasse

STOFFWECHSEL

This shop stocks a vast array of funky and fashionable labels such as Miss Sixty, Firetrap, Only, G-Star and Energie. All you'll ever need to look your best in Berlin's bars and clubs.
🔲 K4 ✉ Dranienburger Strasse 12 ☎ 030 28 87 96 33 🚇 S-Bahn Dranienburger Strasse

Entertainment and Nightlife

B-FLAT

Acoustic music and jazz are on the menu at this downtown club. Drinks are cheaper before 10pm and happy hour is 1am–2am.
🔲 L4 ✉ Rosenthaler Strasse 13 ☎ 030 283 31 23 🚇 S-Bahn Hackescher Markt

PONY BAR

The interior design may be inspired by the 1960s and 1970s, but the music spun here by weekend DJs is up-to-date.
🔲 L4 ✉ Alte Schönhauser Strasse 44 ☎ 030 97 98 47 78 🕐 Mon–Sat 12–late, Sun 6pm–late 🚇 U-Bahn Richard-Luxemburg-Platz

---

MUSIC FOR ALL

Musical tastes have splintered remarkably in recent years; in Berlin this is apparent by the plethora of specialist nightclubs, bebop, house, soul, jungle, ragga, techno and heavy metal–pay your money and take your choice.

SAGE-CLUB

This club in Mitte attracts a diverse collective of fashion-conscious, devotees of clubbing. You can expect everything from rock, big beat, funk, soul and house depending on which night you go. Usually long lines on weekends.
🔲 M6 ✉ Köpenicker Strasse 78 ☎ 030 278 98 30 🕐 Thu from 7pm, Fri, Sat from 11pm, Sun from 11.30pm 🚇 U-Bahn Heinrich-Heine-Strasse

Restaurants

HACKESCHER HOF (€€)

A restaurant-café-wine bar with an old-fashioned appeal and an up-to-the-minute menu and style, rings the changes on continental cuisine from breakfast through to late-night munchies.

➕ L4 ✉ Rosenthaler Strasse 40–41 ☎ 030 283 52 93 🕐 Mon–Fri 7am–3am, Sat–Sun 9am–3am 🚇 S-Bahn Hackescher Markt

LAFIL (€)

This Spanish restaurant is great value for money. The cocktail and wine menus are extensive and the fish and lobster dishes are fantastic.

➕ L3 ✉ Gormannstrasse 22 ☎ 030 28 59 90 26 🕐 Mon–Fri 1pm–2am, Sat–Sun 6pm–2am 🚇 U-Bahn Weinmeisterstrasse

MARE BÊ (€€)

Come here for a gastronomic treat. Reservations are essential at this outstanding French/Italian restaurant.

➕ L4 ✉ Rosenthaler Strasse 46-48 ☎ 030 28 36 545 🕐 Mon–Thu 12–12, Fri 6pm–1am, Sat–Sun 6pm–late 🚇 S-Bahn Hackescher Markt

MIRCHI (€€)

Good food is guaranteed at this Indian and Singaporean fusion restaurant and cocktail bar in Mitte. The lunch menu offers vegetarian, chicken and lamb dishes.

➕ J4 ✉ Oranienburger Strasse 50 ☎ 030 28 44 44 82 🕐 Daily noon–1am 🚇 U-Bahn Oranienburger Tor

OSSENA (€–€€)

Popular Italian restaurant ▷ 56.

➕ L4 ✉ Rosenthaler Strasse 42 ☎ 030 280 998 77 🕐 9am–midnight 🚇 S-Bahn Hackescher Markt

OXYMORON (€€)

Delicious Italian food at the 1920s style lounge in Hackesche Höfe. Also stylish bar and dance floor.

➕ L4 ✉ Rosenthaler Strasse 40–41, Hackesche Höfe ☎ 030 28 39 18 86 🕐 Daily 11am–late, sunset club Wed 10am–midnight (Sep–end Jun), Fri–Sat 11am–late 🚇 S-Bahn Hackescher Markt

SIXTIES (€)

Red, white and blue are the signature colours of a pro-American cuisine eatery that rustles up some pretty decent burgers and fries, steaks, shakes, Tex-Mex tacos and more, in a 1960s-diner setting.

➕ K4 ✉ Oranienburger Strasse 11 ☎ 030 28 59 90 41 🕐 Sun–Thu 10am–2am, Fri–Sat 10am–4am 🚇 S-Bahn Hackescher Markt

TRATTORIA PIAZZA ROSSA (€)

Well-heeled twenty-somethings meet at this eatery in the modern Rathaus Passagen across from the Fernsehturm, for decent Italian fish and meat dishes, and a range of pizzas.

➕ L5 ✉ Rathausstrasse 5 ☎ 030 612 24 29 🕐 Daily 11am–2am 🚇 U- and S-Bahn Alexanderplatz

Cafés

CAFÉ BRAVO (€€)

The two cube-shape areas with mirrored walls and transparent ceilings, form an unusual meeting and eating space at the heart of the Kunstwerke Institute.

➕ K4 ✉ Auguststrasse 69, in der Kunstwerke ☎ 030 283 87 44 40 🕐 Daily 11am–midnight 🚇 U-Bahn Oranienburger Tor

ZUM NUSSBAUM (€)

A traditional Berlin Gasthaus near Fischerinsel in Nikolaiviertel.

➕ L5 ✉ Am Nussbaum 3 ☎ 030 242 30 95 🕐 Daily 12–12 🚇 U-Bahn Klosterstrasse

---

BREAKFAST IN BERLIN

For Berliners, breakfast is a way of life. You can, it seems, take the meal at any time of the day, and you can spend as long over it as you like. Ham and eggs, sausage, cheese, muesli, pumpernickel and even cakes may be on the agenda.

Gentrification proceeds apace in this former East Berlin district, popular with students and ethnic minorities attracted by its low-cost housing, new bars, budget restaurants boutiques and entertainment venues.

Sights	**90–92**	Top 25	**TOP 25**
Shopping	**93**	Kollwitzplatz ▷ **90**
Entertainment and Nightlife	**93**	Husemannstrasse ▷ **91**
Restaurants	**94**	

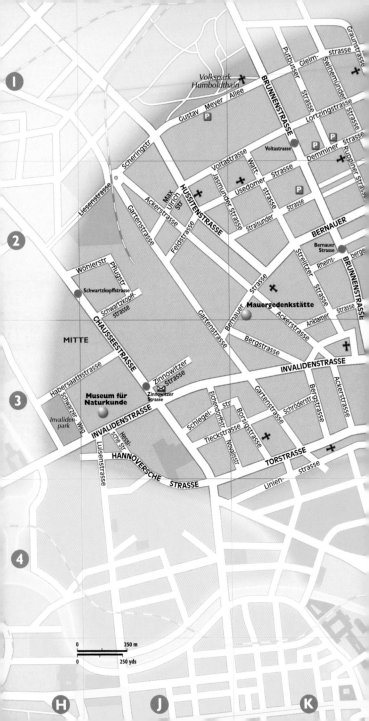

Kollwitzplatz

TOP 25

Now part of a thriving area, Kollwitzplatz is a meeting place for young and old

THE BASICS

🚉 M2
✉ Prenzlauer Berg
Ⓤ U-Bahn Eberswalder Strasse, Senefelderplatz
🚊 Tram M1, M10, M12
🍴 Many ethnic restaurants and cafés

HIGHLIGHTS

● Jüdische Schule
● Wasserturm
● Knaackstrasse
● Prenzlauer Berg Museum (▷ 92)

Named after the artist Käthe Kollwitz (1867–1945), this square in Prenzlauer Berg stands at the heart of a district that has blossomed in recent years. Formerly a rundown part of Communist East Berlin, it has discovered capitalism in a big way.

Mixed images Students, artists and young urban professionals have flocked to Prenzlauer Berg. The district's buildings are a curious mixture: there are a few surviving pre–World War II houses and apartment blocks, some of them still riddled with bullet and shrapnel holes from the Battle of Berlin in 1945; rather more unreconstructed Communist-era edifices, gloomy and shabby-looking, and badly in need of some tender loving care and a lick of paint; and a large stock of brightly painted buildings that have been renovated or rebuilt since the city's reunification. Many renovated buildings can be found in and around Kollwitzplatz.

Jewish character South of Kollwitzplatz, in Rykestrasse, stands the Jüdische Schule (1904), a large former Jewish school, which now houses a Jewish educational foundation. Nearby, the grounds of what was once a Jewish cemetery have been taken over by a children's playground and a new housing and office development. Across the way, a massive Wasserturm (water tower) in a small park is a signature image of the area. Close to the point where Knaackstrasse emerges into Prenzlauer Allee, is the Prenzlauer Berg Museum (▷ 92).

*Cafés have sprung up
along the charming,
wide, tree-lined
Husemannstrasse*

Husemannstrasse

**Lying just north of Kollwitzplatz, this
short street is typical of the transforma-
tion that Prenzlauer Berg has undergone
as gentrification of the district continues.**

Cultured place Husemannstrasse stands at the
heart of the action in Prenzlauer Berg, where many
trendy shops and cafés are taking over the ground
floor areas of renovated post–war apartment blocks.
Among the small-scale cultural foundations in this
area are the Museum Berliner Arbeiterleben
(Museum of Berlin Working Life) at No. 12, which
covers the period around 1900, and the
Prater/Volksbühne theatre in Kastanienallee.
However, the undoubted star of the show is the
Kultur Brauerei (▷ 93), a multifunctional cultural
complex that occupies the handsome old buildings
of a massive former brewery, and which attracts
alternatives-seeking multitudes from around Berlin.
In this foundation are theatres, performance and
practice venues for alternative music and theatre
groups, a cinema multiplex, restaurants, and the
antique commercial design collection of the
Sammlung Industrielle Gestaltung (▷ 92).

Going north At the north end of Husemannstrasse, Danziger Strasse connects with the busy
traffic intersection outside the Eberswalder Strasse
U-Bahn station, where several tram lines also con-
verge. This is on the way to more residential north
Prenzlauer Berg and Pankow, and to the sports
facilities at the Friedrich-Ludwig-Jahn-Sportpark.
Here, the Max Schmelling Halle, is used for
exhibitions and conventions.

THE BASICS

🚆 M2
✉ Prenzlauer Berg
🚇 U-Bahn Eberswalder
Strasse
🚋 Tram M1, M10, M12
🍴 Many ethnic restaurants
and cafés

HIGHLIGHTS

● Museum Berliner
Arbeiterleben
● Kultur Brauerei (▷ 93)
● Sammlung Industrielle
Gestaltung (▷ 92)

More to See

GETHSEMANE KIRCHE

This church, built in 1893, became the spiritual hub of the resistance movement in 1989.

➕ M1 ✉ Stargarder Strasse 77 ☎ 030 44 71 55 67 🚇 U- or S-Bahn Schönhauser Allee

HAMBURGER BAHNHOF

This old station has been converted into an art gallery.

➕ Off map to west ✉ Invalidenstrasse 50–51 ☎ 030 39 78 34 12 🕐 Tue–Fri 10–6, Sat, Sun 11–6 🚇 S-Bahn Hauptbahnhof, Lehrter Bahnhof 🚹 Moderate

MAUERGEDENKSTÄTTE

A section of the Berlin Wall serves as a memorial to those who died. The foundation includes a Documentation Centre and a chapel.

➕ K2 ✉ Bernauer Strasse 111 ☎ 030 464 10 30 🕐 Wed–Sun 10–5 🚇 S-Bahn Nordbahnhof 🚹 Free

MAUERPARK

This section of the former death strip of the Berlin Wall documents Berlin's history since that time.

➕ L1 ✉ Eberswalder Strasse 🚇 U-Bahn Eberswalder Strasse 🚌 Bus 245, 247

MUSEUM FÜR NATURKUNDE (NATURAL HISTORY MUSEUM)

Explore the geology, palaeontology and zoology exhibits. You'll also see the world's largest assembled dinosaur skeleton.

➕ J3 BInvalidenstrasse 43 ☎ 030 20 93 85 91 🕐 Tue–Fri 9.30–5, Sat, Sun 10–6 🚇 U-Bahn Zinnowitzer Strasse, S-Bahn Nordbahnhof 🚹 Moderate

PRENZLAUER BERG MUSEUM

This local museum focuses on the cultural history of the Prenzlauer Berg.

➕ M3 ✉ Prenzlauer Allee 227–228 ☎ 030 902 95 39 16 🕐 Tue, Thu, Sun 10–6 🚇 U-Bahn Senefelderplatz 🚊 Tram M2 🚹 Free

SAMMLUNG INDUSTRIELLE GESTALTUNG

East German design, from the 1950s to the present day.

➕ M2 ✉ Knaackstrasse 97 ☎ 030 44 31 78 68 🕐 Wed–Sun 1–8 🚇 U-Bahn Eberswalder Strasse 🚹 Inexpensive

Graffiti sprayed murals cover this former death strip of the Berlin Wall

Shopping

EISDIELER
A showcase for young Berlin designers.
➕ M2 ✉ Kastanienallee 12 ☎ 030 28 39 12 91 🚇 U-Bahn Oranienburger Tor

FRANZ & JOSEPH SCHEIBEN
The friendly staff will be glad to help you rifle through the racks of rare vinyl and second-hand CDs.
➕ L2 ✉ Kastanienalle 48 ☎ 030 41 71 46 82 🚇 U-Bahn Rosenthaler Platz

GURU-LADEN
Everything you need to give your home an exotic facelift. Printed textiles, Buddhas, sculptural lamps, banana-leaf

THE ALTERNATIVE SCENE

Berlin's chic cosmopolitan image is constantly being undermined by a brazenly nonconformist alternative with roots in the 1960s. There is plenty of evidence of the latter in the remarkable variety of stores specializing in second-hand and offbeat clothing and jewellery. You can have great fun inspecting the wares. A good starting point is the Garage (▷ 47), which sells used clothes by the kilo. The more discerning should head for Kastanienallee.

notebooks and recycled paper products from

India, Nepal, Mexico and Africa.
➕ M1 ✉ Pappelallee 2 ☎ 030 44 01 33 72 🚇 U-Bahn Eberswalder Strasse

DIE ROSE
Designer clothing and accessories from the1920s to the 1970s.
➕ M1 ✉ Schönhauser Allee 57 ☎ 030 92 25 00 25 🚇 U-Bahn Eberswalder Strasse

SERGEANT PEPPERS
The place to shop for authentic 1960s clothing as well as antique clothing including bathing suits.
➕ L2 ✉ Kastanienallee 91–92 ☎ 030 448 11 21 🚇 U-Bahn Eberswalder Strasse

Entertainment and Nightlife

ALBA BERLIN
If you fancy catching the Albatrosses' skills on the basketball court, head for the Max Schlemming Hall, one of the best sports venues in the world. There is one midweek and one weekend match per week all year round.
➕ L1 ✉ Cantianstrasse 24 ☎ 030 300 90 50 🚇 U-Bahn Eberswalder Strasse

KESSELHAUS
Dance nights in a converted former brewery, now known as the Kultur Brauerei, this buzzing

LOCAL TIPPLES

A special local drink is Berliner Weisse, beer with a dash of raspberry or woodruff syrup (*mit Grün*)—addictive if you have a sweet tooth. This is a traditional beverage; more trendy is *Herva mit Mosel,* a peculiar blend of white wine with maté tea that Berliners now consume at least half a million times annually. Hardened drinkers prefer *Korn,* frothy beer with a schnapps chaser.

place accommodates various elements of the alternative cultural scene.
➕ M2 ✉ Knaackstrasse 97 ☎ 030 44 31 50 🕐 Times vary; usually open from 8pm 🚇 U-Bahn Eberswalder Strasse

KNAACK
Concerts, dances, club evenings and private parties, with music from local bands and DJs.
➕ Off map to northeast ✉ Greifswalder Strasse 224 ☎ 030 442 70 61 🕐 Times vary; usually open from 7 or 8pm 🚋 Tram M4

PRENZLAUER BERG

SHOPPING/ENTERTAINMENT AND NIGHTLIFE

Restaurants

PRICES

Prices are approximate, based on a 3-course meal for one person.
€€€   over €30
€€   €15–€30
€   up to €15

MAO THAI STAMMHAUS (€€)

This is universally regarded as the finest Thai restaurant in Berlin, with top-class service and elegant surroundings. It is a bit pricey, but the beautifully presented food is delicious and deserves its excellent reputation.

🚇 M2 ✉ Wörther Strasse 30 ☎ 030 441 92 61 🕐 Daily 12–12 🚇 U-Bahn Senefelderplatz

OFFENBACH-STUBEN (€€)

Something of a rarity—a classic restaurant from the old DDR days. It's still going strong, with its

GOOD VALUE

Compared to many other European capitals, Berlin is a relatively inexpensive place to eat out. Even a fantastic meal in a top-class restaurant is affordable when compared with the equivalent dining experience in Paris or London. However, credit cards are not universally accepted though, so it is probably wise to carry cash with you.

traditional Berlin style and hearty German fare, and a style that runs to old theatrical props and operetta titles for menu items.

🚇 Off map to northeast ✉ Stubbenkammerstrasse 8 ☎ 030 445 85 02 🕐 Daily 6pm–12, or later 🚇 S-Bahn Prenzlauer Allee

OSTWIND (€€)

The Asian cuisine of this fine restaurant covers the Chinese, Thai and Vietnamese kitchens and adds dishes from other countries, yet manages to seem authentic in each genre.

🚇 M2 ✉ Wörther Strasse 30 ☎ 030 441 92 61 🕐 Daily 12–12 🚇 U-Bahn Senefelderplatz

PASTERNAK (€)

Marina Lehmann's lovely restaurant, which serves a wide range of traditional Russian fare, has a literary theme. It is essential to make reservations in advance as it's extremely popular, perhaps for nostalgic reasons, with local people.

🚇 M2 ✉ Knaackstrasse 22–24 ☎ 030 441 33 99 🕐 Daily 10am–midnight 🚇 U-Bahn Senefelderplatz

SODA (€€)

Housed in the vast Kultur Brauerei cultural complex, Soda offers youthful fusion cuisine with plenty of fizz, in a room that's fitted out in a cool modern style, or on an outside terrace in

summer. There's an associated beer garden.

🚇 M2 ✉ Knaackstrasse 97 ☎ 030 44 05 60 71 🕐 Daily 10am–midnight 🚇 U-Bahn Eberswalder Strasse

WEINSTEIN (€€)

Weinstein is one of the best wine bars in the city, with the bonus that it is also a bistro and restaurant. The classic German and French food is very good, but customers are happy to come here simply for the quality wine list and the atmosphere. The elegance and service, reminiscent of the restaurants and brasseries of Paris in the late 19th and early 20th centuries, will make this a meal to remember.

🚇 M1 ✉ Lychener Strasse 33 ☎ 030 441 18 42 🕐 Daily 6pm–2am 🚇 U-Bahn Eberswalder Strasse

HEALTH ON THE MENU

Food scares in Germany and in other countries in Europe may prompt health-conscious Germans to change their eating habits. Traditionally veal and pork have been part of their staple diet but poultry, fish and nonmeat dishes are gaining popularity both at home and in restaurants. The number of Asian and vegetarian establishments has been growing as well.

Berliners are spoiled for choice when it comes time to get away from the stresses of city life. Right on their doorstep there are parks, forests, lakes and pretty villages that make much-loved places of escape.

BERNAU

ZEPERNICK

BUCH

16

E28

109

ESS

SCHWANEBECK

17

1

BUCHHOLZ

KAROW

10

36

71

ESS

158

3

Peckberge

2

E28

158

BLANKENBURG

114

MALCHOW

4

5

109

WARTENBERG

WEISSENSEE

2

HOHEN
SCHÖNHAUSEN

MARZAHN

HÖNOW

**Zeiss Gross
Planetarium**

LICHTENBERG

FRIEDRICHS-
HAIN

1   5

MAHLSDORF

**Eastside
Gallery**

FRIEDRICHS-
FELDE

BIESDORF

Oberbaumbrücke

*Tierpark
Berlin*

NEUKÖLLN

*Treptower
Park*

KARLSHORST

TREPTOW

23

24

96a

FRIEDRICHS-
HAGEN

JOHANNISTHAL

KÖPENICK

*Grosser
Müggelsee*

BRITZ

Teltowkanal

**Schloss
Köpenick**

Dahme

*Britzer
Garten*

179

E36

BUCKOW

GRÜNAU

Müggelturm

**ALT-
GLIENICKE**

RUDOW

LICHTENRADE

BOHNSDORF

Ethnologisches Museum

Exhibits at the Museum of Ethnography (right) include detailed Mayan carvings (left)

THE BASICS

www.smb.museum.de

🔲 Off map to south

✉ Lansstrasse 8, Dahlem

☎ 030 830 14 38

🕐 Tue–Fri 10–6, Sat–Sun 11–6

🍴 Café

🚇 U-Bahn Dahlem-Dorf

🚌 Bus 110, X83, X11

🚆 Lichterfelde West

♿ Good

🎫 Inexpensive

HIGHLIGHTS

● Polynesian clubhouse
● Oceanian boats
● Pre-Columbian gold statuettes
● Peruvian pottery
● Throne and footstool from Cameroon
● Benin bronzes
● Indonesian shadow puppets
● Sri Lankan carved masks
● Australian bark painting
● World music headphones

The folk art theme extends beyond the Ethnological Museum to the nearby Dahlem-Dorf U-Bahn station, where modern primitivist sculptures offer pro-vocative seating. Test them for comfort, then make your own artistic judgment.

Exhibitions Although the airy rooms of the Ethnologisches Museum appear large, there is exhibition space for only a fraction of its 400,000-plus ethnological items. Only Oceania and the Americas are represented by permanent exhibitions. Africa, East Asia and South Asia are covered in temporary displays.

Oceania The Oceanian boats are probably the highlight of the collection. The display includes an 18th-century vessel known as a Tongiaki from Tonga, which resembles a catamaran. For landlubbers there is the fantastically decorated male clubhouse, from the Palau Islands of the western Pacific.

Pre-Columbian art The focus of the American collection is the exhibition of ancient sculptures and figurines, mainly originating from Mexico and Peru. Gold was the medium preferred by many of these artists and the craftsmanship represented here is perhaps among the best of its kind in the world. Just as beautiful, and more arresting, are the decorated stone *stelae* from Cozumalhuapa (Guatemala), which were created to fend off evil spirits.

This Renaissance-style hunting lodge has been used by hunters for over 400 years

Jagdschloss Grunewald

The Grunewald forest is an amazing woodland on the western edge of Berlin. The dreamily scenic 32sq km (12sq miles), dotted with lakes, beaches and nature reserves, are a preferred playground of Berliners at weekends.

Hunting lodge Jagdschloss Grunewald is an attractive Renaissance hunting lodge, built in 1542 for Elector Joachim II of Brandenburg. The stables and outbuildings date from around 1700, when the house was surrounded by a moat. Today the lodge is a museum decorated with paintings and furniture from various royal collections; the chase is the predominant theme. One picture shows Kaiser Wilhelm II on a visit to the Grunewald. The 17th-century Dutch school is well represented among the paintings on display, but the best work is by a German, Lucas Cranach the Elder, who has an entire room to himself. Equally remarkable is the painted wooden ceiling of the Great Hall (Grosser Saal) on the ground floor. Across the courtyard, the barn is now a hunting museum.

Grunewald Forest Paths crisscross the forest, beaches fringe the Havel and there is space for leisure pursuits from boating to hang-gliding. You can swim in the Grunewaldsee, site of the hunting lodge, and in the Krumme Lanke. Between these two lakes is a marshy nature reserve known as the Langes Luch. For views, climb the Grunewaldturm, a 72m (236ft) folly on the banks of the Havel, built in memory of Kaiser Wilhelm I in 1897.

THE BASICS

Jagdschloss Grunewald
➕ Off map to west
✉ Hüttenweg 100, Am Grunewaldsee
☎ 030 813 35 97
🕐 Mid-May to mid-Oct Tue–Sun 10–5; mid-Oct to mid-May Sat, Sun 10–4
🚌 Bus 115, 183, X83
💷 Inexpensive

Grunewaldturm
➕ Off map to west
✉ Havelchaussee 61, Wilmersdorf
☎ 030 300 07 30
🕐 Tower: daily 10–6 (10–midnight in summer)
🍴 Restaurant
🚌 Bus 114, 118, 218, 316, 318, 620
💷 Inexpensive

HIGHLIGHTS

Jagdschloss Grunewald
● Hunting museum
● *Adam and Eve and Judith*, Lucas Cranach the Elder
● *Julius Caesar*, Rubens
● Wooden ceiling in Great Hall

FARTHER AFIELD ★ **TOP 25**

99

Spandau Zitadelle

TOP 25

The 16th-century Zitadelle at Spandau (left). Nikolaikirche in the Altstadt (right)

THE BASICS

www.zitadelle-spandau.de
+ Off map to west
✉ Strasse Am Juliusturm, Spandau
☎ 030 354 94 40
🕐 Tue–Fri 9–5, Sat, Sun 10–5
🍴 Am Juliusturm, (Zitadelle)
Ⓠ U-Bahn Zitadelle
🚌 Bus X33
🚉 Spandau
♿ Few
💷 Inexpensive

HIGHLIGHTS

● Cannons
● Statue of Albrecht the Bear
● Museum of the Middle Ages
● Juliusturm
● Bastion walls
● Old Magazine
● Ruined arsenal
● Kolk

**Of the many attractive villages on Berlin's outskirts, a favourite is ancient Spandau with its redbrick Zitadelle, picturesque streets and views across the Havel.
The best vantage point is the Juliusturm, the oldest surviving part of the Zitadelle.**

The Zitadelle A strategic location at the confluence of the rivers Spree and Havel made Spandau important in the Middle Ages. The first Zitadelle (fortress), dating from the 12th century, was rebuilt by Joachim III in 1557. The oldest surviving part of the building is the crenellated Juliusturm—the view from the top of the tower is worth the steep climb. Most of the bastions and outbuildings date from the 19th century, though the Old Magazine is as ancient as the castle itself.

Many lives One exhibit in the museum at Spandau castle is an 1860 cannon, brought back from Siberia, where it had languished for more than a century. The fortress last saw active service during the Napoleonic Wars, when the Old Arsenal was reduced to ruins. Just inside the castle gateway is the statue of a defiant Albrecht, the famous Bear of Brandenburg.

Altstadt Spandau The attractive Old Town is a short walk from the castle. The Gothic house (Gotisches Haus) in Breite Strasse dates from 1232, and in the Reformationsplatz, the central square, are plenty of cafés and the Nikolaikirche. North of here lies the quaint old area known as the Kolk.

More to See

BOTANISCHER GARTEN (BOTANICAL GARDEN)

More than 18,000 varieties of plants and flowers in beautifully landscaped grounds.

➕ Farther Afield map ✉ Königin-Luise-Strasse 6–8, Dahlem ☎ 030 83 85 01 00 🕐 Daily May–Jul 9–9; Apr, Aug 9–8; Sep 9–7; Mar, Oct 9–6; Feb 9–5; Nov–Jan 9–4 🚉 S-Bahn Botanischer Garten 💷 Moderate

BRITZER GARTEN

Created for the National Garden Show in 1985, the 100ha (247-acre) site is popular with Berliners. There are nature trails, a lake and a restaurant.

➕ Farther Afield map ✉ Sangerhauser Weg 1, Neukölln ☎ 030 700 90 60 🕐 Daily 9–dusk 🚌 Bus M44, 179, 181 💷 Inexpensive

BRÜCKE MUSEUM

This gallery exhibits work from the group of 20th-century German artists known as Die Brücke.

➕ Farther Afield map ✉ Bussardsteig 9, Dahlem ☎ 030 831 20 29 🕐 Wed–Mon 11–5 🚌 Bus 115 💷 Moderate

EASTSIDE GALLERY

Graffiti art as revealed on 730m (2,395ft) of the former Berlin Wall, on the north bank of the River Spree. It is said to be the world's largest open-air art gallery.

➕ Farther Afield map ✉ Mühlenstrasse 🚉 U- and S-Bahn Warschauer Strasse 🚌 Bus 140, 142, 147, 340 💷 Free

FILMPARK BABELSBERG

www.filmpark.de

The hub of Germany's film industry for 90 years, these vast studios were responsible for such classics as *Metropolis* (1927) and *The Blue Angel* (1930). You can enjoy a studio tour and marvel at special effects, while experiencing the cinema of the future at this popular attraction.

➕ Off map to southwest ✉ Grossbeerenstrasse, 14482 Potsdam ☎ 0331 721 27 50; 🕐 Apr–end Oct daily 10–6 💷 Expensive 🚌 Bus 601 from Potsdam train station

FREIZEITPARK TEGEL

Possibly Berlin's best park–certainly its

Adolf Engler's Tropical House at the Botanical Garden

Satirical graffiti in the Eastside Gallery

best for children—with table tennis, rowing, trampolines, volleyball, pedal boats and chess. Pleasure cruisers depart from the Greenwich promenade nearby.

➕ Farther Afield map ✉ An der Malche, Tegel 🚇 U-Bahn Alt-Tegel

GEDENKSTÄTTE HAUS DER WANNSEE KONFERENZ (WANNSEE CONFERENCE CENTRE)

In this innocuous-looking mansion beside the shores of Lake Wannsee, leading Nazis plotted the mass extermination of Europe's 11 million Jews. The exhibition tells the whole horrific story.

➕ Farther Afield map ✉ Am Grossen Wannsee 58–58, Zehlendorf ☎ 030 805 00 10 🕐 Daily 10–6 🚉 S-Bahn Wannsee 🚌 Bus N114 🎫 Free

GEDENKSTÄTTE SACHSENHAUSEN

Some 100,000 prisoners perished at this concentration camp during World War II. The great lie 'Work makes you free', inscribed on the entrance gate, is a chilling reminder of the deception and evil once practiced here. Two museums tell the terrible story of the camp. One focuses on the plight of the Jews; the other, in the former kitchens, displays various objects and other illustrations of daily life.

➕ Off map to northwest ✉ Strasse der Nationen 22 ☎ 033 01 20 00 🕐 Mar–end Oct Tue–Sun 8.30–6; Oct–end Mar 8.30–4 🍴 None 🚉 S-Bahn Oranienburg (then 20-minute walk) 🚉 Oranienburg ♿ Few 🎫 Free

KLEISTGRAB (KLEIST'S GRAVE)

Tucked away in a secluded spot in Wannsee is the grave of the Romantic poet Heinrich von Kleist, who committed suicide here with his mistress in 1811.

➕ Farther Afield map ✉ Bismarckstrasse, Zehlendorf 🚉 S-Bahn Wannsee

MÜGGELTURM AND MÜGGELSEE

This tower, 30m (100ft) high by the Teufelsee, has views of the lake and

The sign on the gates of Sachsenhausen Concentration Camp gave false hope to all who perished here

Action hero at Filmpark Babelsberg (left)

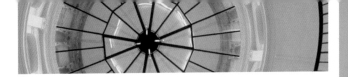

woodlands of the Müggelsee. The nearby Müggelsee, Berlin's largest lake, is a popular place in summer for sunbathing, swimming, windsurfing and other water sports. There's even a sand beach with *Strandkörben* (wicker shelter seats) for rent. At other times, a stroll along its forested banks makes a welcome fresh-air break.

➕ Farther Afield map ✉ Kleiner Müggelberg, Köpenpick ☎ 030 656 98 12 🕐 Daily 8am–dusk 🚌 Bus 169 ✋ Inexpensive

MUSEUMSDORF DÜPPEL

On the site of a village founded around 1170, this open-air museum is a re-creation of a medieval village. Costumed re-enactors afford visitors an insight into life in the Berlin area during the Middle Ages and practise some of the arts, crafts and house-hold activities of the period.

➕ Farther Afield map ✉ Clauerstrasse 11, Zehlendorf ☎ 030 802 66 71 🕐 Easter–early Oct Sun and hols 10–5, Thu 3–7 🚉 S-Bahn Mexikoplatz, then bus 118 ✋ Inexpensive; guided tours: expensive

MUSEUM FÜR INDISCHE KUNST; OSTASIATISCHE KUNST (MUSEUMS OF INDIAN & EAST ASIAN ART)

These two museums exhibit the art and culture of India and the Far East.

➕ Farther Afield map ✉ Lansstrasse 8 ☎ 030 830 14 38 🕐 Tue–Fri 10–6, Sat–Sun 11–6 🚉 U-Bahn Dahlem-Dorf ✋ Inexpensive

OBERBAUMBRÜCKE

More than 500 different kinds of tiles were used in the renovation of what was once Berlin's longest bridge.

➕ Farther Afield map ✉ Mühlenstrasse 🚉 U-Bahn Schlesisches Tor

OLYMPIASTADION (OLYMPIC STADIUM)

This famous stadium was built to host the 1936 Olympics. The giant bell tower (*Glockenturm*), rises to 77m (253ft).

➕ Farther Afield map ✉ Olympische Platz 3 ☎ 030 30 06 33; guided tours 030 30 68 81 00 🚉 S- and U-Bahn Olympiastadion ✋ Inexpensive

The Oberbaumbrücke is an imposing city sight

More to See in Potsdam

SCHLOSS CECILIENHOF

www.spsb.de

North of Potsdam, set in parkland called Neuer Garten (New Garden), is Schloss Cecilienhof, built for Crown Prince Wilhelm, Kaiser Wilhelm II's son. Completed in 1917, it is an early 20th-century reproduction of a half-timber English Tudor manor house. In the summer of 1945, Cecilienhof was the setting for the Potsdam Conference, when US President Harry S. Truman, Soviet Political Leader Joseph Stalin and British Prime Minister Winston Churchill met to shape the fate of the postwar world. Cecilienhof is now a luxury hotel.

🚫 Off map to southwest ✉ Neuer Garten ☎ 0331 969 42 44 🕐 Apr–end Oct Tue–Sun 10–5; Nov–end Mar Sat, Sun 10–4 🍴 Restaurant 🚇 S-Bahn Potsdam-Stadt 🚌 Bus 694; tram 92 🚆 Potsdam-Stadt ✋ Moderate

SANSSOUCI

www.spsg.de

On the western edge of Potsdam you'll find landscaped Sanssouci Park.

It contains two quite different yet equally impressive palaces built for Frederick the Great. Formal gardens, terraces, fountains and follies complete the picture. Schloss Sanssouci was designed by Georg Wenzeslaus von Knobelsdorff. The single-storey rococo façade, topped by a shallow green dome, conceals a succession of gorgeously furnished rooms and a collection of precious objects. The best view of the expansive redbrick façade of New Palace (Neues Palais) is from the imposing driveway. Johann Büring designed the façade, and Karl von Gontard the sumptuous interior. About a dozen of the palace's more than 200 rooms are open to visitors.

🚫 Off map to southwest ✉ Maulbeerallee, Potsdam ☎ 0331 969 42 02 🕐 Schloss Sanssouci: Apr–end Oct Tue–Sun 9–5; Nov–end Mar Tue–Sun 9–4; New Palace: Apr–end Oct Tue–Sun 9–12.30, 1–5; Nov–end Mar Tue–Sun 9–12.30, 1–4 🍴 Café; restaurant 🚇 S-Bahn Potsdam-Stadt 🚌 Bus 695; tram 96, 98 🚆 Wild Park ♿ Few ✋ Park: free; Schloss: expensive (guided tour only); New Palace: moderate

Schloss Cecilienhof is a touch of England in a foreign land

KLEIN-GLIENICKE

www.spsg.de

The mock-Renaissance Schloss was designed in 1824 by Karl Friedrich Schinkel for Prince Friedrich Karl of Prussia, the brother of Kaiser Wilhelm I. Nowadays the grounds are known for their arcadian follies and ornamental garden. The follies are by Schinkel, and the park was laid out by Peter Lenné, also responsible for the Berlin Tiergarten. The themes of Renaissance Italy and Classical Greece can be detected among the follies. The most extraordinary flight of fancy must be the Klosterhof, with genuine Italian remains from Venice and from Pisa. Just outside the gate is the Glienicker Bridge. The bridge came to the world's attention in 1962 when, marking the border between East and West, it was the scene of a swap involving the US pilot Gary Powers, who had been shot down by the Soviet air force on allegations of spying. The bridge subsequently starred in films and became a symbol of the Cold War.

🚩 Off map to southwest ✉ Königstrasse 36 ☎ 0331 969 42 02 🕐 Park: daily 7am–8pm Schloss: 15 May–15 Oct Sat–Sun 10–5 🍴 Excellent restaurant 🚇 S-Bahn Wannsee 🚌 Bus 116 🚉 Potsdam-Stadt ♿ None 💰 Inexpensive

ALTER MARKT

The Alter Markt (Old Market) is the hub of Potsdam, with the Nikolaikirche at its heart. Crown Prince Friedrich Wilhelm IV commissioned the building but had to wait until his father passed away before completing the project and adding the distinguished dome to the roof. The 18th-century baroque Altes Rathaus (Old City hall), adorned with a gilded figure of Atlas, forms part of the Potsdam's city walls. Framing the remaining sides of the market square are a large 1970s structure and parts of the Stadtschloss (City Castle), which was badly damaged during World War II and then demolished by city planners in 1959.

🚩 Off map to southwest ✉ Am Alten Markt 🚇 S-Bahn Potsdam Stadt

Sumptuous Schloss Sanssouci has fine rococo detail and lavishly furnished rooms

More to See

SCHLOSS KÖPENICK

Standing in peaceful parkland on the Schlossinsel, at the confluence of the Dahme and Spree, this elegant, 17th-century former residence of the rulers of the Mark Brandenburg houses a mnuseum of decorative arts.

➕ Off map to southeast ✉ Schlossinsel, Köpenpick ☎ 030 65 66 17 48 ⏰ Tue–Sun 10–6 🍴 Café ☷ S-Bahn Köpenick 🚌 Bus 167, 169, 360 🚢 Köpenick ✋ Inexpensive

TIERPARK BERLIN-FRIEDRICHSFELDE

One of Berlin's two zoos, on the east side of the city in grounds that once formed part of Schloss Friedrichsfelde. Concerts and other events are held in the restored palace.

➕ Off map to east ✉ Am Tierpark 125 ☎ 030 51 53 10 ⏰ Daily 9–dark ☷ U-Bahn Tierpark

TREPTOWER PARK

The largest green space on the eastern side of the city spreads out along the banks of the River Spree. Fairs and other events are often held here.

➕ Off map to east ✉ Puschkinallee ☷ S-Bahn Treptower Park

VOLKSPARK JUNGFERNHEIDE

This large park, on the northern edge of Charlottenburg, offers swimming, boat rental, hiking, sports fields and a theatre.

➕ Off map to north west ✉ Saatwinkler Damm ☷ U-Bahn Siemensdamm

WANNSEE–KLADOW FERRY

The enjoyable ferry ride from Wannsee to Kladow is inexpensive (free with a *Tageskarte*).

➕ Off map to southwest ✉ Wannsee Pier 🚢 BVG Line F10

ZEISS-GROSSPLANETARIUM

Berlin has three planetariums and observatories. Children will love the interesting monthly shows that are put on here.

➕ Off map to northeast ✉ Prenzlauer Allee 80 ☎ 030 42 18 45 12 ⏰ Shows: Mon–Fri 9.30, 11; also afternoons on Wed, Sat, Sun ☷ S-Bahn Prenzlauer Allee ✋ Expensive

Treptower Park is a great place to relax and glimpse the city

Berlin caters to all, having a good selection of budget, mid-range and luxury hotels, as well as inexpensive hostels. If you're looking for a good quality hotel, it's usually best to reserve a room in advance.

Introduction

The steadily increasing number of visitors to Berlin has brought with it rapid growth and investment in the city's hotel industry, mainly in the luxury market. Good-quality mid-range and budget hotels tend to book up fast, but there is also an excellent selection of well-equipped hostels.

Location

Most of the luxury hotels, business hotels and chain hotels are concentrated around Mitte, the Kurfürstendamm and Savignyplatz, but you can get some good deals farther out. Berlin's public transportation system is efficient and extensive, so unless you are beyond the limits of the city and the S-Bahn you will be just a half-hour's journey away from anything you want to see. Budget hotels and hostels tend to be on side streets, but they are never far from public transport links.

Extra costs

The average price of a hotel room in Berlin is lower than in many other major European cities. Most hotels have a breakfast buffet, which can be simply *Kaffee und Schrippen* (coffee and rolls) with cheese and cold meats, or a feast of smoked meats, fresh fruit and cake. Breakfast is often not included in the price of a room in luxury and mid-range hotels, but is included in budget hotels and hostels. You can book hotels through the website www.berlin-tourist-information.de.

FINDING A ROOM

Rooms can be booked in advance through the Berlin tourism website www.berlin-tourist-information.de or through the hotel finder at www.germany-tourism.co.uk. The best place to start your search once you're in situ is at the local tourist office, which may offer a room-finding service for a nominal fee. If the tourist office is closed, there's often a noticeboard outside with a list of nearby hotels and—if you're lucky—a map. If not, just take a stroll round the middle of town.

Berlin caters to all accommodation needs from simple hotels to grand, luxury establishments

Budget Hotels

PRICES

Expect to pay between €80 and €95 for a budget hotel.

A & O FRIEDRICHSHAIN

www.aohotels.de
Inexpensive rooms in the old east end. Multilingual staff, cut-price meals and bike rental.
🔳 Off map to east
✉ Boxhagener Strasse 73
☎ 030 29 77 81 26
🚇 S-Bahn Ostkreuz

BERLINER CITY-PENSION

www.berliner-city-pension.de
In the heart of Mitte in Alexanderplatz. Rooms in this renovated hotel are clean and light.
🔳 Off map to east
✉ Proskauer Strasse 13
☎ 030 42 08 16 15
🚇 S-Bahn Storkower Strasse

CIRCUS

www.circus-berlin.de
Central hostel popular with backpackers. Luggage store, bike rental, ticket service and 24-hour reception.
🔳 L4 ✉ Rosa-Luxemburg-Strasse 39–41 ☎ 030 28 39 14 33 🚇 U-Bahn Rosa-Luxemburg-Platz

CITY HOSTEL BERLIN

www.meininger-hostels.de
Great value for money, this stylish hostel has no curfew and offers a huge breakfast.
🔳 J8 ✉ Hallesches Ufer 30 ☎ 030 66 63 61 00

🚇 U-Bahn Möckernbrücke Bartholdy Platz

FRAUEN HOTEL ARTEMISIA

www.frauenhotel-berlin.de
Just for women—with 12 attractive rooms, a bar and a library. In Wilmersdorf. Book early.
🔳 B8 ✉ Brandenburgische Strasse 18 ☎ 030 873 89 05
🚇 U-Bahn Konstanzer Strasse

HOTEL-PENSION AM SCHLOSS BELLEVUE

www.hotelamschlossbelle-vue.de
A family-run hotel in a central yet quiet location not far from the Kurfürstendamm.
🔳 F4 ✉ Paulstrasse 3
☎ 030 391 12 27 🚇 U-Bahn Turmstrasse

HOTEL-PENSION MÜNCHEN

www.hotel-pension-muenchen-in-berlin.de
Modern sculptures and paintings by local artists

YOUTH HOSTELS

Youth hostels (*Jugendgästehäuser* or *Jugendherbergen*) do not impose restrictions on age or families. You need to be a member of the Youth Hostel Association (YHA) and you can buy a membership card from your own national YHA or on arrival at the youth hostel. For reservations and further information, log onto www.djh-ris.de, which has an English version.

grace this lodging in the Wilmersdorf district, two U-Bahn stops south of Kurfürstendamm. The artist owner keeps it clean and personable. Room types range from single without bathroom to 4-person apartments with.
🔳 D9 ✉ Güntzelstrasse 62
☎ 030 857 91 20 🚇 U-Bahn Güntzelstrasse

HOTEL TRANSIT LOFT

www.transit-loft.de
This is one of the best hotels in the lower price range. Transit Loft has 47 clean rooms and surprisingly good facilities.
🔳 Off map to northeast
✉ Greifswalder Strasse 219, entrance at Immanuelkirchstrasse 14a
☎ 030 48 49 37 73
🚇 U-Bahn Senefelderplatz

INTERMEZZO–HOTEL FÜR FRAUEN

www.hotelintermezzo.de
This small, down-to-earth hotel is exclusively for women. Boys up to 12 can stay here, too.
🔳 J6 ✉ Gertrud-Kolmar-Strasse 5 ☎ 030 22 48 90 96
🚇 U-Bahn Mohrenstrasse

PEGASUS HOSTEL

www.pegasushostel.de
This hostel has more to offer than most—a garden, excellent cooking facilities, apartments and the choice of private or communal showers.
🔳 Off map to east
✉ Strasse der Pariser Kommune 35 ☎ 030 297 73 60 🚇 S-Bahn Ostbahnhof

Mid-Range Hotels

WHERE TO STAY | MID-RANGE HOTELS

PRICES

Expect to pay between €95 and €185 for a mid-range hotel.

ALAMEDA-BERLIN

www.alameda.de
Relax after sightseeing in this rooftop haven in the heart of the city. The light, spacious rooms, which take up a top-floor conversion, have sloping ceilings, arched windows, balconies and great views. The hotel is within walking distance of the major sights around Mitte and close to regular public transportation links.
➕ M6 ✉ Michaelkirchstrasse 15 ☎ 030 30 86 83 30
🚇 Heinrich-Heine-Strasse

ARTE LUISE KUNSTHOTEL

www.kuenstlerheim.de
Different well-known artists have designed each room in this hotel for art buffs, built in 1825 as a city mansion. It now has a striking façade, a lobby filled with sculptures, a large hall used for exhibitions, and philosophical maxims decorating the main stairway.
➕ J4 ✉ Luisenstrasse 19 ☎ 030 28 44 80 🚇 U- and S-Bahn Friedrichstrasse

BERLIN EXCELSIOR HOTEL

www.hotel-excelsior.de
Duplex suites, garden terrace, 317 rooms and several restaurants and bars. Well-placed near the zoo station.
➕ D6 ✉ Hardenbergstrasse 14 ☎ 030 315 50 🚇 U- or S-Bahn Zoologischer Garten

BERLIN PLAZA HOTEL

www.plazahotel.de
This hotel, near the Ku'damm, has 131 rooms and a terrace restaurant.
➕ C7 ✉ Knesebeckstrasse 63 ☎ 030 88 41 34 44
🚇 U-Bahn Uhlandstrasse

BOULEVARD

www.ahc-hotels.com
This hotel offers excellent service, clean and spacious rooms and is just off the Kurfürstendamm and close to the action, making it great value for money. The hotel's main selling point is its rooftop café terrace, a great spot

HOTEL MEINEKE

The 60 high-ceilinged rooms of this comfortable hotel are decorated in an old-fashioned bourgeois style, with a modern art touch. A carpeted staircase leads to the first-floor reception desk and the breakfast room is hung with contemporary art. Although this mid-price hotel is in the side street of Meinekestrasse, at No. 10, just 200m (220 yards) from the Ku'damm, it's quiet.
➕ D7 ☎ 030 80 31 90; www.markhotels.de
🚇 U-Bahn Kurfürstendamm

for admiring the view on a summer's evening.
➕ D7 ✉ Kurfürstendamm 12 ✉ 030 88 42 50 🚇 U- or S-Bahn Zoologischer Garten, Kurfürstendamm

FJORD HOTEL

www.fjordhotelberlin.de
Clean and modern, this 57-room hotel is convenient for the Kulturforum. Roof terrace open for breakfast in summer.
➕ H7 ✉ Bissingzeile 13 ☎ 030 25 47 20 🚇 U-Bahn Mendessohn-Bartholdy-Park

HANSABLICK

www.hotel-hansablick.de
On a quiet side street beside the Spree, this hotel has warm, small rooms with a slightly chintzy modern style, some with a river view and balcony, in a townhouse that dates from around 1900. A handsome lounge contains original works of art.
➕ E5 ✉ Flotowstrasse 6 ☎ 030 390 48 00 🚇 U-Bahn Hansaplatz; S-Bahn Tiergarten

HONIGMOND GARDEN HOTEL

www.honigmond-berlin.de
The main attraction of this small family hotel in the heart of the Scheunenviertel is its beautiful garden and intimate surroundings. You can sit outside during the summmer under the umbrellas and palms.
➕ J3 ✉ Invalidenstrassse 98 ☎ 030 28 44 55 77 🚇 S-Bahn Nordbahnhof

HOTEL ASTORIA

www.hotel-astoria.de
This 32-room hotel is among the art galleries of Fasanenstrasse. Bar and babysitting service.
🞤 D6 ✉ Fasanenstrasse 2
☎ 030 312 40 67 🚇 U- or S-Bahn Zoologischher Garten

HOTEL JURINE

www.hotel-jurine.de
This friendly, family-run hotel is close to Prenzlauer Berg. All 49 bright and airy rooms have pay and satellite TV.
🞤 K3 ✉ Schwedter Strasse 15 ☎ 030 443 29 90
🚇 U-Bahn Senefelderplatz

HOTEL RIEHMERS HOFGARTEN

www.riehmers-hofgarten.de
This florid stucco apartment house was built in 1891 for prosperous Berliners. 20 good-size rooms.
🞤 J8 ✉ Yorckstrasse 83
☎ 030 78 09 88 00
🚇 U-Bahn Mehringdamm

HOTEL VILLA KASTANIA

www.villakastania.de
Comfortable hotel in Charlottenburg. The 47 rooms have good facilities, and there is a pool.
🞤 Off map to west
✉ Kastanienallee 20 ☎ 030 30 00 20 🚇 U-Bahn Theodor-Heuss-Platz

LUISENHOF

www.luisenhof.de
In an elegant, restored town house built in 1822, the graceful Luisenhof manages to be both close to the heart of the action in Mitte and tranquil at the same time. The rooms are bright and modern yet still retain an element of the house's original character.
🞤 M6 ✉ Köpenicker Strasse 92 ☎ 030 246 28 10 🚇 U-Bahn Märkisches Museum

PENSION SAVOY

www.hotel-pension-savoy.de
The Pension Savoy is in the west of the city off the Kurfürstendamm. An impressive entrance hall with baroque-style columns and a marble floor greets you as you enter this friendly guesthouse. Each of the 20 guest rooms has modern amenities including cable TV, telephone, hair dryer and safety deposit box, as well as a bathroom with bath or shower. Bicycles to rent.
🞤 D7 ✉ Meinekestrasse 4
☎ 030 88 47 16 10
🚇 U-Bahn Kurfürstendam

WHERE TO LOOK

Berlin offers a surprising variety of lower-priced accommodation and you do not necessarily need to trek out to the backwoods. Schöneberg and Kreuzberg districts both have a plentiful supply of pensions and simple hotels, most of which are clean and up to scratch. Young people may prefer to stay in Kreuzberg for its lively night scene.

RESIDENZ BERLIN

www.hotel-residenz.com
Jugendstil architecture is one of the boasts of this 80-room hotel near the Ku'damm. Restaurant.
🞤 D7 ✉ Meinekestrasse 9
☎ 030 88 44 30 🚇 U-Bahn Kurfürstendamm

SAVOY HOTEL-PENSION

www.hotel-pension-savoy.com
An impressive entrance-hall with baroque-style columns and a marble floor awaits you as you enter this friendly guesthouse. The rooms are well looked after and neatly furnished. Bicycles are available for rent.
🞤 D7 ✉ Meinekestrasse 4
☎ 030 88 47 16 10
🚇 U-Bahn Kurfürstendamm

TIERGARTEN BERLIN

www.hotel-tiergarten.de
Effortlessly combines the efficiency of a modern business hotel and more than a little of the charm of a privately owned lodging with local character, in an early 1900s building with courtyard just north of the Spree.
🞤 F4 ✉ Alt-Moabit 89
☎ 030 39 98 96 🚇 U-Bahn Turmstrasse

LA VIE HOTEL JOACHIMSHOF

www.la-vie-hotels.de
Comfortable and modern 35-room hotel, opposite the Natural History Museum. Small bar, restaurant and sauna.
🞤 J3 ✉ Invalidenstrassse 98
☎ 030 203 95 61 00
🚇 U-Bahn Zinnowitzer Strasse

Luxury Hotels

PRICES

Expect to pay from €185 or more for a luxury hotel.

BERLIN HILTON
www.hilton.de
In a great location this hotel has 500 rooms, plus bars, restaurants, fitness area, pool and fabulous views over the Gendarmenmarkt. All rooms have Internet access and TV.
⊞ K6 ⊠ Mohrenstrasse 30 ☎ 030 20 23 42 55 ⊚ U-Bahn Stadtmitte

DORINT AM GENDARMENMARKT
www.dorint.de
This hotel has dark marble and frosted glass in its classy rooms and guests can enjoy views of the Gendarmenmarkt.
⊞ K5 ⊠ Charlottenstrasse 50–52 ☎ 030 20 37 50 ⊚ U-Bahn Stadtmitte

GRAND HOTEL ESPLANADE
www.esplanade.de
The last word in luxury and comfort, in rooms from large doubles all the way up to the stellar penthouse suite, many of them affording fine city views. A quintet of eating and drinking options includes Harry's New York Bar and the restaurant Vivo (▷ 48).
⊞ F7 ⊠ Lützowufer 15 ☎ 030 25 47 80 ⊚ U-Bahn Kurfürstenstrasse

GRAND HYATT
www.hyatt.com
This hotel has city views, 340 rooms, a swimming pool and fitness centre.
⊞ H6 ⊠ Marlene-Dietrich-Platz 2 ☎ 030 25 53 12 34 ⊚ U- or S-Bahn Potsdamer Platz

HOTEL ADLON KEMPINSKI BERLIN
www.hotel-adlon.de
This historic 337-room hotel, at the Brandenburg Gate is one of the city's most luxurious.
⊞ J5 ⊠ Unter den Linden 77 ☎ 030 22 61 11 11 ⊚ S-Bahn Unter den Linden

HOTEL BRANDEN-BURGER HOF
www.brandenburger-hof.com
Stylish late 19th-century building, near the Kaiser Wilhelm Memorial Church. Winter garden restaurant. 82 rooms.
⊞ E7 ⊠ Eislebener Strasse 14 ☎ 030 21 40 50 ⊚ U-Bahn Augsburger Strasse

INTER-CONTINENTAL BERLIN
www.berlin.intercontinental.com
The city's most glamorous hotel has 510 rooms, 70 suites, a swimming pool, sauna and a business facility.
⊞ F6 ⊠ Budapester Strasse 2 ☎ 030 260 20 ⊚ U- or S-Bahn Zoologischer Garten

KEMPINSKI HOTEL BRISTOL BERLIN
www.kempinski.com
Chandeliers and deep carpets are a constant reminder of this hotel's resplendent past. Courteous service. There are 315 rooms and 44 suites. Fitness room and swimming pool.
⊞ D7 ⊠ Kurfürstendamm 27 ☎ 030 88 43 40 ⊚ U-Bahn Uhlandstrasse

SAVOY HOTEL
www.hotel-savoy.com
This is an elegant hotel with a large roof terrace and many of the amenities of the city's top hotels but with more user-friendly rates. It is just a few minutes' walk from the Ku'damm.
⊞ D6 ⊠ Fasanenstrasse 9–10 ☎ 030 31 10 30 ⊚ U- and S-Bahn Zoologischer Garten

---

HOTEL LOCATIONS

You can stay virtually anywhere in Berlin, but the mid-range hotels tend to cluster around the Ku'damm. Business hotels and luxury hotels tend to be in Mitte. Charlottenburg and Schöneberg are quieter yet equally convenient. The establishments spawned by the East German authorities, such as the Forum on Alexanderplatz, are trying desperately to cope with the chill winds of economic competition. The most scenic locations are Tegel, Wannsee, the Grunewald forest and Müggelsee.

Use this section to help you in planning your visit to Berlin and getting around once you are there. You will also find useful tips and a section on language.

Planning Ahead

When to Go

Expect rain at any time. Summer can be hot and humid. April to June is the most comfortable period to vist. The arts scene is liveliest between October and May. From late November up to Christmas the city is lighted up with decorations and the streets are filled with markets.

AVERAGE DAILY MAXIMUM TEMPERATURES

JAN	FEB	MAR	APR	MAY	JUN	JUL	AUG	SEP	OCT	NOV	DEC
35°F	39°F	47°F	54°F	65°F	70°F	73°F	73°F	66°F	56°F	45°F	38°F
1°C	3°C	8°C	12°C	18°C	21°C	22°C	22°C	18°C	13°C	7°C	3°C

Spring (mid-March to end May) is extremely pleasant, with flowers and trees coming into bloom throughout the parks and along the avenues.

Summer (June to early September) can be hot with the occasional dramatic thunder storm.

Autumn (mid-September to end November) is comfortable, but changeable with fine bright weather often preceded by periods of drizzle and grey skies.

Winter (December to mid-March) is extremely cold with occasional snowfalls, but it is common to experience crisp, bright days.

WHAT'S ON

On any given day, Berlin has around 250 exhibitions and more than 400 independent theatre groups, 170 museums, 200 art galleries and 150 auditoriums. Check the listings magazines.

January *6-Day Race*: Cycling event at the Velodrom, Landsberger Allee.

February *International Film Festival (Berlinale)*: The world's filmmakers come to Potsdamer Platz.

May *German Women's Open*: Tennis tournament.

June *Fête de la Musique*: Concerts (from rock to classical) at Brandenburg Gate, Hackesche Höfe and other open-air venues.

Christopher Street Day: Gay and lesbian procession.

July *Love Parade*: 'The largest rave party in the world'. Involving 1.5 million young people. Strasse des 17 Juni, Tiergarten.

August *Lange Nacht der Museen*: More than 100 museums are open after midnight.

September *Berliner Festwochen*: A month of opera, music, theatre and painting throughout the city.

September/October *Berlin Marathon*.

October *German Unity Day* (3 Oct): Street festivals on Unter den Linden.

November *Jazz Festival Berlin*: Jazz concerts are held citywide.

December *Christmas Markets*: All month at Opernpalais (Unter den Linden 5), Breitscheidplatz, Alexanderplatz, Winterfeldplatz (Sunday only) and Spandau Altstadt.

New Year: Celebrations at the Brandenburg Gate and a gala evening at Staatsoper.

Useful Websites

www.berlin-tourist-information.de
The official site for the Berlin tourist board with details of hotels, sightseeing, guided tours and current events. You can order theatre and concert tickets online and make hotel bookings from their list of approved hotels. In English and German.

www.berlin.de
The city of Berlin's official site with details of all the current events in both English and German.

www.berlinOnline.de
A site providing information on life in the city with news, jobs, current events, clubbing, shopping and ticket information. In German only.

www.meinberlin.de
A German-only site focusing on the cultural and leisure activities in Berlin.

www.freshmilk.de
A creative site in German only dedicated to multimedia, modern art and culture from video and cinema to music and exhibitions.

www.tip-berlin.de
The official German language site for the listings magazine *Tip*, detailing the major events and what is going on in the city in the way of films, music and partying in the month ahead.

www.zitty.de
In German only, the official site for the listings magazine *Zitty*, reviewing the top films, restaurants and bars in Berlin.

www.taz.de
The site of Berlin newspaper *Das Tagesspiegel*, in German, with all the latest news and views.

www.bvg.de
Useful site in English and German giving information on travelling around the city.

PRIME TRAVEL SITES

www.fodors.com
A complete travel-planning site. You can research prices and weather; book air tickets, cars and rooms; ask questions (and get answers) from fellow travellers; and find links to other sites.

www.tripadvisor.com
Promises unbiased reviews and recommendations of hotels, resorts, vacations and guides and lists the top attractions and hotels in major cities across the globe.

INTERNET CAFÉS

easyInternetCafé
E7 Kufürstendamm 224 030 88 70 79 70
6am–1am
U-Kurfürstendamm

alpha Internet Café
M1 Dunckerstrasse 72 030 447 90 67
Mon–Fri 12–1am, Sat–Sun 2pm–1am
S-Bahn Prenzlauer Allee

Surf and Sushi
K4 Oranienburger Strasse 17
030 28 38 48 98
12–late
S-Bahn Hackescher Markt

Getting There

ENTRY REQUIREMENTS

For the latest passport and visa information, look up the embassy website at www.london.diplo.de or www.germany.info/relaunch/index.html

INSURANCE

EU nationals receive reduced medical treatment with the new EHIC card—obtain this card before travelling. Full health and travel insurance is still advised. US travellers should check their health coverage before departure and buy a supplementary policy as necessary.

AIRPORTS

Berlin has three international airports: Tegel, 8km (5 miles) to the northwest of central Berlin; Schönefeld, 18km (11 miles) to the southeast; and Tempelhof, 4km (2.5 miles) to the south. Tempelhof handles all domestic and charter flights.

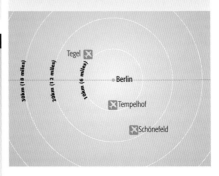

ARRIVING AT TEGEL AIRPORT

Off map to northwest. For airport information ☎ 0180 500 0186. The airport is linked to the city via the bus network. Bus 109 from the airport will take you to Zoo Station and bus X9 goes to the Kurfürstendamm (30 min). Bus 128 goes to the north of Berlin, while the TXL bus goes as far as the government district. A taxi right into the city costs around €19 and takes around 20 minutes.

ARRIVING AT SCHÖNEFELD AIRPORT

Off map to southwest. For airport information ☎ 0180 500 0186. There is a free shuttle transfer from the terminal building to Berlin-Schönefeld airport station. The Airport Express takes passengers from the airport to the Kurfürstendamm (30 min). The 171 bus links the terminal building with the Rudow U-Bahn station and the U7 line. A taxi to the city costs around €33 and takes around 40 minutes.

ARRIVING AT TEMPELHOF AIRPORT

Off map to southeast. For airport information ☎ 0180 500 0186. Direct U-Bahn links

between Platz der Luftbrücke station at the airport mean that you can reach the heart of the city in 10–20 minutes. Take the U-Bahn line 6 from Platz der Luftbrücke (not Tempelhof) into the city. Change at Friedrichstrasse for the western side of the city. A taxi to central Berlin costs around €17 and takes around 15 minutes.

ARRIVING BY BUS
Berlin's central bus station (ZOB) is on Masurenallee opposite the International Conference Centre (ICC) in the district of Charlottenburg. For travel information ☎ 030 302 53 61/030 30 10 01 75 (24 hour). For tickets call 030 301 03 80 (Mon–Fri 6am–9pm, Sat–Sun 6–3).

ARRIVING BY TRAIN
There are good connections from major European cities. The city's main station for international and long-distance services is the Berlin Hauptbahnhof. Other city stations handle regional and local services. For train information: Deutsche Bahn AG (German National Railway) ➕ D6 ✉ Hardenbergplatz 11 ☎ 11 8 61 (24 hour), www.bahn.de

ARRIVING BY CAR
A ring road provides access from the north and south and southern and eastern road links are currently being improved and modernized. If you intend to bring your car into central Berlin, find a hotel with parking as there are few car parks and little on-street parking.

CUSTOMS

VISITING FROM ANOTHER EU COUNTRY:
3200 cigarettes or
400 cigarillos or 200 cigars or
3kg of smoking tobacco
10 litres of spirits or 20 litres of fortified wine (such as port of sherry) or
90 litres of wine (of which only 60 litres can be sparkling wine) or110 litres of beer

VISITING GERMANY FROM OUTSIDE THE EU:
200 cigarettes or
100 cigarillos or 50 cigars or
250g of smoking tobacco
1 litre of spirits or strong liquers
2 litres of still table wine or 2 litres of fortified wine, sparkling wine or other liquers
50cc perfume
250cc/ml of eau de toilette

Getting Around

POTSDAM BOUND

To do a side trip to historic Potsdam (▷ 104–105), the quickest way to get there under your own steam from the city is to take S-Bahn line S1. It passes through the heart of Berlin and you can catch it at stops that include Hackescher Markt, Unter den Linden and Potsdamer Platz.

VISITORS WITH DISABILITIES

Berlin has a wheelchair breakdown service, Der Rollstuhlpannendienst, that can be called out around the clock and will come out to fix any problems on the spot like the AA or AAA breakdown service ☎ 030 84 31 09 10, www.rollstuhlpann-endienst.de

Buses have rear-door access and safety straps for wheelchairs. Wheelchair users may find the Mobilcab service useful: Telebus-Zentrale ➕ E7 ✉ Joachimstaler Strasse 17 ☎ 030 21 29 72 00

Berlin has an excellent public transport network, with two urban rail services and numerous bus and tram routes. The local transport authority is the Berliner Verkehrs-Betriebe (BVG).

● BVG Information Service. Timetables and tickets ☎ 030 194 49; www.bvg.de
● S-Bahn Berlin GmbH Information Service ☎ 030 29 74 33 33; www.s-bahn-berlin.de

TYPES OF TICKET

● The 24-hour ticket (*Tageskarte*) and the weekly *7-Tage-Karte* allow unlimited travel on the BVG network (trains, buses, trams and the ferry from Wannsee to Kladow). The weekly ticket covers unlimited travel during any seven-day period from validation until midnight on the seventh day.
● A single one-way ticket (*Einzelfahrausweis*) is valid for two hours. You can transfer or interrupt your travel.
● The *Kurzstrecke* (short-distance ticket) is valid on the U- and S-Bahn for up to three stops including transfers, or for six stops only (bus/tram).
● BerlinWelcomeCard entitles one adult and up to three children age 6–14 to free BVG travel for three days as well as reductions on sightseeing trips, museums and theatres. Ask at your hotel, tourist information offices or U-Bahn ticket offices.
● Children under 14: reduced-rate travel; children under 6: free.

THE METRO

● The U-Bahn (underground railway) and S-Bahn (city railway), are interchangeable.
● You must buy a ticket from station foyers or from vending machines on platforms. Validate your ticket at a machine on the platform before boarding the train. Routes are referred to by the final stop on the line.
● Trains run every 5 or 10 minutes, Mon–Fri 5am–midnight; Sat–Sun (approximately) 4am–2am. On Friday and Saturday there is a

24-hour service on several city trains and underground lines that runs every 15 minutes.

● You may take bicycles on the U-Bahn on weekdays between 9am and 2pm and after 5.30pm, and all weekend. Cyclists may travel on the S-Bahn at any time. There is a small charge payable.

BUSES

● Central Bus Station, Funkturm ☎ 030 302 5361/030 30 10 01 75

● Enter cream double-decker buses at the front and leave by the doors in the middle or at the back. Pay the driver with small change or show ticket (see above). Multiple tickets, also valid for U- and S-Bahn, can be bought from vending machines at some bus stops or at U-Bahn stations, but not from the driver.

● Route 100 is particularly useful, departing from Zoo Station every 10 minutes and linking the West End with Unter den Linden and Alexanderplatz.

● More than 70 night buses operate half-hourly from 1am to 4am. Line N19 runs through the city every 15 minutes.

STRASSENBAHNEN

● Trams operate largely in eastern Berlin. Ticket procedures are the same as for buses.

MAPS AND TIMETABLES

● Obtain timetables and maps from large U-Bahn ticket offices such as Alexanderplatz ☎ 030 194 49; www.bvg.de

TAXIS

● Taxis are good value, with stands throughout the city. Only use cabs with a meter.
● There is a small surcharge for baggage.
● Not all drivers know their way, so travel with your own map.
● Central taxi call centres ☎ 0800 44 33 222 or 0800 222 22 55
● Chauffeur service ☎ 030 21 09 08 80
● Bike taxis (rickshaws) ☎ 030 93 95 83 46

BGV FERRIES

BVG ferry lines in the Wannsee and Köpenick areas include services from Wannsee to Kladow, Glienicker Bridge to Sacrow, Grünau to Wendenschloss and around the Müggelsee.

CAR SHARING

Visitors can telephone a Mitfahrzentrale (ride centre) to arrange a lift to other German cities in a private car (rates to be agreed beforehand). The Mitfahrzentrale is located at:
Liebland, U-Bahn Zoo, platform 2 ✚ E6 ☎ 030 194 40 (Mon–Fri 9–8, Sat–Sun 10–6)

NEED TO KNOW GETTING AROUND

Essential Facts

● UK ✉ Unter den Linden 32–34 ☎ 030 20 45 70
● US ✉ Neustädtische Kirchstrasse 4–5 ☎ 030 238 51 74

EUROS

The euro is the official currency of Germany. Bank notes in come in denominations of 5, 10, 20, 50, 100, 200 and 500 euros and coins in denominations of 1, 2, 5, 10, 20 and 50 cents and 1 and 2 euros.

10 euros

50 euros

200 euros

500 euros

CUSTOMS REGULATIONS

For details of duty-free allowances for visitors from within the EU and from countries outside the Eu, see 'Customs' panel page 117.

ELECTRICITY

● 220 volts on a two-pin plug.

LOST PROPERTY

● Police, Tempelhof ✚ Off map to southeast ✉ Platz der Luftbrücke 6 ☎ 030 75 60 31 01
● BVG Transport Lost and Found ☎ 25 62 30 40

MEDICINES

● Take any specially prescribed medications with you. Check on the generic name of any drugs before you leave home.

MEDICAL AND DENTAL TREATMENT

● There are plenty of English-speaking doctors in Berlin. For a referral service telephone the medical emergency number.
● Emergency numbers (within Berlin):
Medical ☎ 31 00 31
Dental ☎ 89 00 43 33
Poison ☎ 030 192 40

MONEY MATTERS

● Exchange offices (*Wechselstuben*) can be found all over Berlin: Zoo station (Bahnhof Zoo) ✚ D6 ⏰ Mon–Sat 7.30–10pm, Sun and holidays 8–7; Friedrichstrasse station ✚ J5 ⏰ Mon–Fri 7am–7.30pm, Sat–Sun 8–4; holidays 9–2.
● Automatic cash dispensers (ATMs) can be found citywide.
● Most major credit cards are recognized but not widely accepted.
● Euro traveller's cheques are preferred, but those in US dollars are acceptable.
● American Express Offices:
✚ E7 ✉ Bayreutherstrasse 37
☎ 030 21 47 62 92
✚ K5 ✉ Friedrichstrasse 172
☎ 030 20 45 57 21

OPENING HOURS
- **Shops** 🕐 Mon–Fri 9.30–6.30, Sat 9–2. On Thursday some shops stay open until 8pm.
- **Banks** 🕐 Mon–Fri 9–12.30. Afternoons vary
- **Pharmacies** 🕐 Mon–Fri 9.30–6.30, Sat 9–2
☎ 030 31 00 31 for night pharmacies.

STUDENT TRAVELLERS
- Discounts on public transport, in museums and some theatres are available with an International Student Identity Card.
- European 'Transalpino' tickets are also available for people under 26.

SENSIBLE PRECAUTIONS
- Although Berlin is one of the safer European cities, always remain on your guard. Keep a close eye on bags and do not hang them on the back of chairs in restaurants.
- Avoid poorly lighted areas, some places such as Oranienburger Strasse can become seedy red-light districts at night.
- Keep wallets and purses concealed when travelling on the U-Bahn and trams.

TELEPHONES
- In phone boxes marked Kartentelefon use phone cards, available from post offices, petrol stations and newspaper kiosks.
- Boxes marked International and telephones in post offices are for long-distance calls.
- Calls are cheapest after 10pm and on Sundays.
- Follow the dialling instructions (in several languages) in the box.
- To call the UK from Berlin dial 0044, then omit the first 0 from the area code.
- To call Berlin from the UK dial 0049 30, then the number.
- To call the US from Berlin dial 001. To call Berlin from the US dial 01149 30, then the number.
- Local information 11833; international 11834

EMERGENCY PHONE NUMBERS
- Coins are not needed for emergency calls from public telephones: Police ☎ 110; Fire ☎ 112; Ambulance ☎ 115
- American Hotline: crisis hotline and free, recorded medical referral service ☎ 0177 8141510

SIGHTSEEING TOURS
BBS Berliner Bären Stadtrundfahrt
Daily tours and days out in eight languages. Departures from Ku'damm and Alexanderplatz. ☎ 030 35 19 52 70

Berolina Stadtrundfahrten
Daily bus tours of Berlin and Potsdam–Sanssouci in eight languages. Departures from the Ku'damm at Meinekestrasse ☎ 030 88 56 80 30

Severin and Kühn
Circular city tour and excursions farther afield. Departures from Kurfürstendamm, at the corner of Fasanenstrasse ☎ 880 41 90; www.severin-kuehn-berlin.de

PUBLIC HOLIDAYS

● 1 January; Good Friday; Easter Monday; 1 May; Ascension Day; Pentecost Monday; 3 October (German Unity Day); Christmas Day; 26 December.

POST OFFICES

● Alte Potsdamer Strasse 7 🕓 Mon–Fri 9am–8pm, Sat 9am–4pm

✉ Nürnberger Strasse 8 🕓 Mon–Fri 8am–6pm, Sat 8am–1pm

● Stamps can be bought from vending machines on the Ku'damm, as well as from post offices.

● Postboxes are bright yellow.

TOILETS

● Men's toilets are labelled *Herren*, women's *Damen* or *Frauen*.

● Public toilets are free but scarce. Use those in cafés, restaurants, hotels and department stores.

TOURIST INFORMATION OFFICES

● Tourist Info Center, Europa-Center 🚩 E7 ✉ Budapester Strasse 45 🕓 Mon–Sat 10–7, Sun 10–6 🚇 S- or U-Bahn Zoologischer Garten.

● Tourist Info Café Unter dem Fernsehturm ✉ Alexanderplatz 🕓 Daily 10–6 🚇 S- or U-Bahn Alexanderplatz.

● Brandenburg Gate 🕓 Daily 10–6 🚇 S- or U-Bahn Unter den Linden

● Berlin Tourismus Marketing GmbH (office) ✉ Am Karlsbad 11 ☎ 030 25 00 25; www.berlin-tourist-information.de

WOMEN TRAVELLERS

● Schokofabrik (Women's Centre): 🚩 Off map to southeast ✉ Marianenstrasse 6 ☎ 030 615 24 40 🕓 Café: Mon–Fri 1pm–12, Sun 12–2pm. Turkish bath: Sun–Fri 11–10.

PLACES OF WORSHIP

Religious services information ☎ 01157	
Protestant	Kaiser Wilhelm Memorial Church (➤ 32) ☎ 030 218 50 23 🕓 Services Sun 10am, 6pm
	Berliner Dom (➤ 77) ☎ 030 20 26 91 11 🕓 Services Sun 10am, 6pm, (Evensong in English Thu 6pm)
Roman Catholic	Hedwigskirche (➤ 68) ☎ 030 203 48 10 🕓 Mass Sun 8am, 10am, 12, 6pm, Sat 7pm
Anglican	St. George's 🚩 Off map to west ✉ Preussenallee 🕓 Morning service 10am. Holy Communion Sun 8am;
Liberal Jewish	Synagogue Pestalozzistrasse 🚩 D6 ✉ Pestalozzistrasse 14 ☎ 030 313 84 11 🕓 Services Fri 7pm, Sat 9.30am
Orthodox Jewish	Adass Jisroel 🚩 J4 ✉ Tucholsky Strasse 40 🕓 Services Fri 5pm; Sat 9.30am

Language

BASICS:

ja	yes
nein	no
bitte	please
danke	thank you
guten Morgen	good morning
guten Abend	good evening
gute Nacht	good night
auf Wiedersehen	goodbye
heute	today
gestern	yesterday
morgen	tomorrow
die Speisekarte	menu
das Frühstück	breakfast
das Mittagessen	lunch
das Abendessen	dinner
der Weisswein	white wine
der Rotwein	red wine
das Bier	beer
das Brot	bread
die Milch	milk
der Zucker	sugar
das Wasser	water
die Rechnung	bill
das Zimmer	room
offen	open
geschlossen	closed
wieviel?	how much?
teuer	expensive
billig	cheap
sprechen Sie Englisch?	do you speak English?
Ich spreche kein Deutsch	I don't speak German
Ich verstehe nicht	I don't understand
Entschuldigen Sie	Excuse me
der Bahnhof	train station
der Flughafen	airport
die Bank	bank
das Postamt	post office
die Polizei	police
das Krankenhaus	hospital

USEFUL WORDS

klein	small
gross	large
schnell	quickly
kalt	cold
warm	hot
gut	good

Potsdamer Platz

123

Timeline

A BERLIN FIRST

Werner Siemens and Johann Georg Malske manufacture the first telegraph in a house on Schöneberger Strasse.

THE WALL

In 1961 200,000 people escaped the GDR in the East and fled to the West, 152,000 of them via Berlin. On the night of 12th August 1961 the GDR closed the border, erecting a wall of barbed wire, concrete slabs and stones to halt the flow of refugees. This was followed by the building of the Wall, a concrete structure 12km (7.5 miles) long. The border was heavily guarded and during the time the Wall stood 152 people lost their lives trying to escape.

Left to right: Frederick the Great; detail of the crest of the German Unification flag; Hitler enters Sudetenlnad, 1938; WW II commemorative plaques at the 1936 Olympic Stadium; signs at former Checkpoint Charlie; entrance to the 1936 Olympic Stadium

1244 First recorded mention of Berlin.

1369 Berlin becomes a member of the Hanseatic League trading association.

1443 Frederick II of Brandenburg builds the first Berlin castle (Schloss).

1448 Berliners defend their privileges in the 'Berliner Unwille' revolt.

1618–48 Berlin is devastated by Austrian and Swedish armies during the Thirty Years' War. The population is halved to less than 6,000.

1701 Elector Frederick III proclaims himself King Frederick I of Prussia. In 1740 Frederick the Great becomes king.

1806 Napoleon enters Berlin.

1848 Germany's 'bourgeois revolution' sees demands for greater middle-class representation in government. Workers take to the barricades.

1871 Berlin becomes capital of a united German Empire under Kaiser Wilhelm I and the Prime Minister of Prussia, Prince Otto von Bismarck.

1918 After the end of World War I, Kaiser Wilhelm II abdicates to make way for a German Republic.

_1920s_ Despite growing social and economic instability, Berlin becomes a cultural powerhouse. Grosz, Einstein, Brecht and Gropius flourish.

_1933_ Hitler becomes German Chancellor.

_1936_ Berlin hosts the Olympic Games.

_1938_ On the 'night of breaking glass' the Nazis orchestrate the destruction of Jewish properties and synagogues.

_1939–45_ World War II.

_1945_ Berlin lies in ruins, its population reduced from 4 million to 2.8 million.

_1945–89_ A city divided (▷ side panel).

_1989_ On 9 November the collapse of communism in Eastern Europe leads to the opening of the Berlin Wall and its eventual demise.

_1990_ Germany is unified.

_1999_ The first session of the Bundestag in the reopened Reichstag building.

_2000_ Berlin once again becomes the capital of a united Germany.

_2002_ Germany adopts the euro.

_2006_ Germany hosts the soccer World Cup.

A CITY DIVIDED

1945 Berlin is divided into four zones of occupation, administered by French, British, US and Soviet forces.

1948–49 A Soviet attempt to force the Western Allies to withdraw from Berlin by blockading the city is foiled by a gigantic airlift of supplies.

1949 Germany is divided into the Federal Republic and the communist German Democratic Republic. Berlin is stranded in the GDR.

1953 Construction workers in East Berlin, protesting at low wages, provoke a full-scale uprising, which is put down by Soviet tanks.

1961 The flood of East Germans to the West is staunched by the building of the Berlin Wall.

1963 John F. Kennedy demonstrates American support for West Berlin in his famous 'Ich bin ein Berliner' speech.

Index

Berlin's
25 BEST

WRITTEN BY Christopher and Melanie Rice
ADDITIONAL WRITING George McDonald
DESIGN CONCEPT AND DESIGN WORK Kate Harling
INDEXER Marie Lorimer
REVIEWING EDITOR Jacinta O'Halloran
SERIES EDITOR Paul Mitchell

ISBN 978-1-4000-1757-7

FIFTH EDITION

IMPORTANT TIP
Time inevitably brings changes, so always confirm prices, travel facts, and other perishable information when it matters. Although Fodor's cannot accept responsibility for errors, you can use this guide in the confidence that we have taken every care to ensure its accuracy.

SPECIAL SALES
This book is available for special discounts for bulk purchases for sales promotions or premiums. Special editions, including personalized covers, excerpts of existing books, and corporate imprints, can be created in large quantities for special needs. For more information, write to Special Markets/Premium Sales, 1745 Broadway, MD 6–2, New York, NY 10019 or email specialmarkets@randomhouse.com.

First published 1997
Colour separation by Keenes
Printed and bound by Leo, China
10 9 8 7 6 5 4 3 2

A03491
Maps in this title produced from mapping © MAIRDUMONT / Falk Verlag 2007
Transport map © Communicarta Ltd, UK

The Automobile Association would like to thank the following photographers and companies for their assistance in the preparation of this book.

Abbreviations for the picture credits are as follows – (t) top; (b) bottom; (c) centre; (l) left; (r) right; (AA) AA World Travel Library

Inside front cover images: **1** AA/Jonathan Smith; **2** AA/Clive Sawyer; **3** AA/Simon McBride; **4** AA/Tony Souter; **5** Bauhaus-archive; **6** AA/Simon McBride; **7** AA/Simon McBride; **8** AA/Simon McBride; **9** AA/Clive Sawyer; 10 AA/Clive Sawyer.

1 AA/Simon McBride; **2-18t** AA/Doug Traverso; **4l** AA/Tony Souter; **5c** AA/Simon McBride; **6cl** AA/Simon McBride; **6cc** AA/Jonathan Smith; **6cr** AA/Simon McBride; **6bl** AA/Simon McBride; **6br** AA/Clive Sawyer; **7cl** AA/Simon McBride; **7cc** AA/Jonathan Smith; **7cr** AA/Clive Sawyer; **7bl** AA/Clive Sawyer; **7bc** AA/Clive Sawyer; **7br** AA/Jonathan Smith; **10ctr** AA/Simon McBride; **10cr** Photodisc; **10cbr** AA/Tony Souter; **10/11b** AA/Tony Souter; **11ctl** AA/Tony Souter; **11cl** AA/Simon McBride; **11cbl** AA/Tony Souter; **12b** Photodisc; **13ctl** AA/Tony Souter; **13cl** AA/Clive Sawyer; **13cbl** AA/Simon McBride; **13bl** AA/Tony Souter; **14ctr** AA/Jonathan Smith; **14cr** AA/Jonathan Smith; **14cbr** AA/Simon McBride; **14br** AA/Jonathan Smith; **15b** AA/Tony Souter; **16ctr** AA/Jonathan Smith; **16cbr** AA/Simon McBride; **16br** AA/James Tims; **17ctl** AA/Clive Sawyer; **17cl** Digital Vision; **17cbl** AA/Jonathan Smith; **17bl** AA/Jonathan Smith; **18ctr** Image 100; **18cr** AA/Tony Souter; **18cbr** AA/Tony Souter; **18br** AA/Clive Sawyer; **19a** (top down) AA/Clive Sawyer; **19b** AA/Simon McBride; **19c** AA/Jonathan Smith; **19d** AA/Adrian Baker; **19e** AA/Jonathan Smith; **19f** AA/Jonathan Smith; **19g** AA/Adrian Baker; **19h** AA/Simon McBride; **20/21** AA/Simon McBride; **24** AA/Clive Sawyer; **25t** AA/Jonathan Smith; **25cl** AA/Tony Souter; **25cr** AA/Tony Souter; **26t** AA/Jonathan Smith; **26bl** AA/Tony Souter; **26br** AA/Jonathan Smith; **27t** AA/Tony Souter; **27c** AA/Jonathan Smith; **28** AA/Simon McBride; **29** AA/Simon McBride; **32l** AA/Doug Traverso; **32r** AA/Tony Souter; **33l** AA/Simon McBride; **33r** AA/Simon McBride; **34l** EPA Photo/DPA/Tim Brakemeier; **34r** AA/Tony Souter; **35** AA/Adrian Baker; **36** Photodisc; **37** AA/Jonathan Smith; **38** AA/Jonathan Smith; **39** AA/Jonathan Smith; **42tl** AA/Jonathan Smith; **42-43t** AA/Jonathan Smith; **42cl** AA/Jonathan Smith; **42cr** AA/Jonathan Smith; **43cl** AA/Jonathan Smith; **43r** AA/Jonathan Smith; **44l** Bauhaus-archive; **44r** Bauhaus-archive; **45t** AA/Jonathan Smith; **45b** Filmmuseum Berlin/Hans Scherhaufer; **46** AA/Adrian Baker; **47t** AA/Michelle Chaplow; **47c** Digital Vision; **48** AA/Tony Souter; **49** AA/Simon McBride; **52** Guy Moberly/Alamy; **53** Silke Reents; **54t** AA/Jonathan Smith; **54bl** AA/Adrian Baker; **54br** AA/Adrian Baker; **55t** Photodisc; **55c** Photodisc; **56** AA/Tony Souter; **57** AA/Jonathan Smith; **60l** AA/Tony Souter; **60r** AA/Clive Sawyer; **61l** AA/Tony Souter; **61c** AA/Tony Souter; **61r** AA/Simon McBride; **62** AA/Clive Sawyer; **62/63** AA/Clive Sawyer; **64l** AA/Jonathan Smith; **64c** AA/Clive Sawyer; **64r** AA/Jonathan Smith; **65l** AA/Simon McBride; **65r** AA/Simon McBride; **66l** AA/Jonathan Smith; **66-67t** AA/Simon McBride; **66cr** AA/Tony Souter; **67l** AA/Jonathan Smith; **67r** AA/Jonathan Smith; **68l** AA/Simon McBride; **68r** AA/Tony Souter; **69t** AA/Jonathan Smith; **69bl** AA/Simon McBride; **69br** Flughafen Berlin Tempelhof; **70** AA/Paul Kenward; **71** Brand X Pics; **72** AA/Clive Sawyer; **73** AA/Tony Souter; **76l** AA/Simon McBride; **76c** AA/Jonathan Smith; **76r** AA/Jonathan Smith; **77l** AA/Clive Sawyer; **77r** AA/Simon McBride; **78l** AA/Simon McBride; **78/79t** AA/Simon McBride; **78cr** AA/Tony Souter; **79tr** AA/Tony Souter; **79cl** AA/Adrian Baker; **79cr** AA/Simon McBride; **80l** AA/Clive Sawyer; **80r** AA/Clive Sawyer; **81l** AA/Simon McBride; **81c** AA/Jonathan Smith; **81r** AA/Simon McBride; **82-83t** AA/Jonathan Smith; **82bl** AA/Clive Sawyer; **82br** AA/Tony Souter; **83bl** AA/Adrian Baker; **83br** AA/Clive Sawyer; **84** AA/Adrian Baker; **85t** AA/Simon McBride; **85c** Brand X Pics; **86** AA/Eric Meacher; **87** AA/Tony Souter; **90** Silke Reents; **91l** AA/Clive Sawyer; **91r** AA/Adrian Baker; **92t** AA/Jonathan Smith; **92b** Silke Reents; **93t** AA/Clive Sawyer; **93c** Photodisc; **94** AA/Clive Sawyer; **95** AA/Simon McBride; **98l** AA/Tony Souter; **98r** AA/Tony Souter; **99** AA/Tony Souter; **100l** AA/Clive Sawyer; **100r** AA/Adrian Baker; **101-103t** AA/Jonathan Smith; **101bl** AA/Adrian Baker; **101br** AA/Simon McBride; **102bl** Andreas T Feuer; **102br** AA/Clive Sawyer; **103b** Silke Reents; **104-105t** AA/Simon McBride; **104b** AA/Jonathan Smith; **105b** AA/Simon McBride; **106t** AA/Jonathan Smith; **106b** AA/Tony Souter; **107** AA/Jonathan Smith; **108-112t** AA/Clive Sawyer; **108ctr** AA/Jonathan Smith; **108cr** AA/Jonathan Smith; **108cbr** AA/Pete Bennett; **108br** AA/Jonathan Smith; **113** AA/Jonathan Smith; **114-125t** AA/Simon McBride; **117b** AA/Simon McBride; **118b** AA/Tony Souter; **119b** AA/Tony Souter; **120c** ECB; **121b** AA/Tony Souter; **123c** AA/Max Jourdan; **123b** AA/Jonathan Smith; **124bl** AA; **124bc** AA/Doug Traverso; **124br** Illustrated London News; **125bl** AA/Adrian Baker; **125bc** AA/Tony Souter; **125br** AA/Adrian Baker.

Every effort has been made to trace the copyright holders, and we apologise in advance for any accidental errors. We would be happy to apply the corrections in the following edition of this publication.